COMPLETE COOKERY

Quick & Easy

DP

DEMPSEY
PARR

This is a Dempsey Parr book
First published in 2000

Dempsey Parr is an imprint of
Parragon
Queen Street House
4 Queen Street
Bath BA1 1HE, UK

ISBN: 1-84084-959-2

Printed in Italy

Note
Cup measurements in this book are for American cups.
Tablespoons are assumed to be 15 ml. Unless otherwise stated,
milk is assumed to be whole, eggs are large,
and pepper is freshly ground black pepper.

Contents

Introduction

This book is designed to appeal to anyone who wants a wholesome but quick and easy diet, and includes many recipes suitable for vegetarians and vegans. Its main aim is to show people that, with a little forethought, it is possible to spend very little time in the kitchen while still enjoying appetizing food. The recipes collected together come from all over the world; some of the Indian and barbecue dishes featured require marinating, often overnight, but it is worth remembering that their actual cooking time is very short once the marinade has been absorbed. The more exotic dishes on offer are balanced by some traditional dishes which are sure to firm family favorites. If you want fast food for everyday meals, or you are short on time and want to prepare a tasty dinner party treat, there is something for everybody in this book.

To save time in the kitchen, always make sure that you have the requisite basics in your cupboard. By keeping a stock of staple foodstuffs such as rice, pasta, spices, and herbs, you can easily turn your hand to any numberof these recipes.

Keeping a full Store-cupboard

Flour

You will need to keep a selection of flour: Self-rising and Whole wheat are the most useful. You may also like to keep some rice flour and cornstarch for thickening sauces and to add to cakes, cookies, and puddings. Buckwheat, garbanzo bean, and soya flours can also be bought. These are useful for combining with other flours to add different flavors and a variety of textures.

Grains and Rice

A good variety of grains is essential. For rice, choose from long-grain, basmati, Italian risotto, short-grain, and wild rice. Look out for fragrant Thai rice, jasmine rice, and combinations of different varieties to add color and texture to your dishes. When choosing your rice, remember that brown rice is a better source of vitamin B1 and fiber.

Other grains add variety to the diet. Try to include some barley millet, bulghur wheat, polenta, oats, semolina, sago, and tapioca.

Pasta

Pasta is very popular nowadays, and there are many types and shapes to choose from. Keep a good selection, such as basic lasagne sheets, tagliatelle, fettuccine (flat ribbons), and spaghetti. For a change, sample some of the many fresh pastas now available. Better still, make your own – hand-rolling pasta can be very satisfying, and you can buy a special machine for rolling the dough and cutting certain shapes.

Legumes

Legumes are a valuable source of protein, vitamins, and minerals. Stock up on soya beans, navy beans, red kidney beans, cannellini beans, garbanzo beans, lentils, split peas, and butter beans. Buy dried legumes for soaking and cooking yourself, or canned varieties for speed and convenience.

Herbs

A good selection of herbs is important for adding variety to your cooking. Fresh herbs are preferable to dried, but it is essential to have dried ones in stock as a useful back-up. You should store dried basil, thyme, bay leaves, oregano, rosemary, mixed herbs, and bouquet garni.

Chilies

These come both fresh and dried and in many colors. The hotness varies so use with caution. The seeds are hottest and are usually discarded. Chili powder should also be used sparingly. Check whether the powder is pure chili or a chili seasoning or blend, which should be milder.

Nuts and seeds

As well as adding protein, vitamins, and useful fats to the diet, nuts and seeds add important flavor and texture to vegetarian meals. Make sure that you keep a good supply of nuts such as hazelnuts, pine nuts, and walnuts. Coconut is useful too.

For your seed collection, have sesame, sunflower, pumpkin, and poppy. Pumpkin seeds in particular are a good source of zinc.

Dried fruits

Currants, raisins, golden raisins, dates, apples, apricots, figs, pears, peaches, prunes, papayas, mangoes, figs, bananas, and pineapples can all be purchased dried and can be used in lots of different recipes. When buying dried fruits, look for untreated varieties: for example, buy figs that have not been rolled in sugar, and choose unsulfured apricots, if they are available.

Oils and fats

Oils are useful for adding subtle flavorings to foods, so it is a good idea to have a selection in your store-cupboard. Use a light olive oil for cooking and extra-virgin olive oil for salad dressings. Use sunflower oil as a good general-purpose oil. Sesame oil is wonderful in stir-fries; hazelnut and walnut oils are superb in salad dressings. Oils and fats add flavor to foods, and contain the important fat-soluble vitamins A, D, E, and K. Remember all fats and oils are high in calories, and that oils are higher in calories than butter or margarine.

Vinegars

Choose three or four vinegars – red or white wine, cider, light malt, tarragon, sherry, or balsamic vinegar, to name just a few. Each will add its own character to your recipes.

Mustards

Mustards are made from black, brown, or white mustard seeds which are ground and mixed with spices. Meaux mustard is made from mixed mustard seeds and has a grainy texture with a warm, taste. Dijon mustard, made from husked and ground mustard seeds, has a sharp flavor. Its versatility in salads and with barbecues makes it ideal for the vegetarian. German mustard is mild and is best used in Scandinavian and German dishes.

Bottled sauces

Soy sauce is widely used in Eastern cookery and is made from fermented yellow soya beans mixed with wheat, salt, yeast, and sugar. Light soy sauce tends to be rather salty, whereas dark soy sauce tends to be sweeter. Teriyaki sauce gives an authentic Japanese flavoring to stir-fries. Black bean and yellow bean sauces add an instant authentic Chinese flavor to stir-fries.

STORING SPICES

Your basic stock of spices should include fresh gingerroot and garlic, chili powder, turmeric, paprika, cloves, cardamom, black pepper, ground coriander, and ground cumin. The powdered spices will keep very well in airtight containers, while the fresh gingerroot and garlic will keep for 7-10 days in the refrigerator. Other useful items, to be acquired as your repertoire increases, are cumin seeds (black as well as white), onion seeds, mustard seeds, cloves, cinnamon, dried red chilies, fenugreek, vegetable ghee and garam masala (a mixture of spices that can either be bought ready-made or made at home in quantity for use whenever required).

USING SPICES

You can use spices whole, ground, roasted, fried, or mixed with yogurt to marinate meat and poultry. One spice can alter the flavor of a dish and a combination of several can produce different colors and textures. The quantities of spices shown in the recipes are merely a guide. Increase or decrease them as you wish, especially in the cases of salt and chili powder, which are a matter of taste.

Many of the recipes in this book call for ground spices, which are generally available in supermarkets as well as in Indian and Pakistani grocers. In India whole spices are ground at home, and there is no doubt that freshly ground spices do make a noticeable difference to the taste.

Some recipes require roasted spices. In India, this is done on a thawa, but you can use a heavy, ideally cast-iron skillet. No water or oil is needed: the spices are simply dry-roasted whole while the pan is shaken to stop them burning on the bottom.

Remember that long cooking over a lowish heat will improve the taste of the food as it allows the spices to be absorbed. This is why re-heating dishes the following day is no problem for most Indian food.

USEFUL ORIENTAL INGREDIENTS

Bamboo shoots
These are added for texture, as they have very little flavor. Available in cans, they are a common ingredient in Chinese cooking.

Beansprouts
These are mung bean shoots, which are very nutritious, containing many vitamins. They add crunch to a recipe and are widely available. Do not overcook them, as they wilt and do not add texture to the dish.

Black beans
These are soy beans and are very salty. They can be bought and crushed with salt and then rinsed or used in the form of a ready-made sauce for convenience.

Chinese beans
These long beans may be eaten whole and are very tender. green beans may also be used.

Chinese five-spice powder
An aromatic blend of cinnamon, cloves, star anise, fennel, and brown peppercorns. It is often used in marinades.

Chinese leaves
A light green leaf with a sweet flavor. It can be found readily in most supermarkets.

Hoisin sauce
A dark brown, sweet, thick sauce that is widely available. It is made from spices, soy sauce, garlic, and chili and is often served as a dipping sauce.

Lychees
These are worth buying fresh, as they are easy to prepare. Inside the inedible skin is a fragrant white fruit. Lychees are available canned and are a classic Chinese ingredient.

Mango
Choose a ripe mango for its sweet, scented flesh. If a mango is underripe when bought, leave it in a sunny place for a few days before using.

Noodles
The Chinese use several varieties of noodle. You will probably find it easier to use the readily available dried varieties, such as egg noodles, which are yellow, rice-stick noodles, which are white and very fine, or transparent noodles, which are opaque when dry and turn transparent on cooking. However, cellophane or rice noodles may be used instead.

Oyster sauce
Readily available, this sauce is made from oysters, salt, seasonings, and cornstarch and is brown in color.

Pak choi
Also known as Chinese cabbage, this has a mild, slightly bitter flavor.

Rice vinegar
This has a mild, sweet taste that is quite delicate. It is available in some supermarkets, but if not available use cider vinegar instead.

Rice wine
This is similar to dry sherry in color, alcohol content, and smell, but it is worth buying rice wine for its distinctive flavor.

Sesame oil
This is made from roasted sesame seeds and has an intense flavor. It burns easily and is therefore added at the end of cooking for flavor, and is not used for frying.

Soy sauce
This is widely available, but it is worth buying a good grade of sauce. It is produced in both light and dark varieties – the former is used with fish and vegetables for a lighter color and flavor, while the latter, being darker, richer, saltier, and more intense, is used as a dipping sauce or with strongly flavored meats.

Star anise
This is an eight-pointed, star-shaped pod with a strong aniseed flavor. The spice is also available ground. If a pod is added to a dish, it should be removed before serving.

Szechuan pepper
This is quite hot and spicy and should be used sparingly. It is red in color and is readily available.

Tofu or bean curd
This soya bean paste is available in several forms. The cake variety, which is soft and spongy and a white-gray color, is used in this book. It is very bland, but adds texture to dishes and is perfect for absorbing all the other flavors in the dish.

Water chestnuts
These are flat and round and can usually only be purchased in cans, already peeled. They add a delicious crunch to dishes and have a sweet flavor.

Yellow beans
Again a soy bean and very salty. Use a variety that is chunky rather than smooth.

Soups & Appetizers

Soups are an important part of Italian cuisine. They vary in consistency from light and delicate appetizers to hearty main meal soups. Although some may be puréed the ingredients never lose their delicious flavor.

Antipasto means 'before the main course' and what is served may be simple and inexpensive or highly elaborate. It usually comes in three categories: meat, fish, and vegetables. There are many varieties of cold meats, including ham, invariably sliced paper thin. All varieties of fish are enjoyed by the Italians, fresh sardines are particularly popular. Cook vegetables only until 'al dente' and still slightly crisp so that they retain more nutrients and the colors remain bright.

Use plenty of color – bell peppers, snow peas, and baby-corn-on-the-cobs are all readily available. Use Italian staples, such as extra-virgin olive oil and balsamic vinegar for a salad dressing, and sprinkle over Italian cheeses, such as Parmesan and Pecorino.

This chapter also contains a range of delicious side dishes which will complement your main meal. Whatever you are looking for to tempt those tastebuds, you are sure to find it among these delicious delicacies.

Green Soup

*This fresh-tasting soup with dwarf beans, cucumber, and watercress
can be served warm or chilled on a hot summer day.*

Serves 4

INGREDIENTS

1 tbsp olive oil
1 onion, chopped
1 garlic clove, chopped
7 oz potato, peeled and cut into
1 inch cubes

scant 3 cups vegetable or chicken
stock
1 small cucumber or $^1/_2$ large
cucumber, cut into chunks

3 oz bunch watercress
$4^1/_2$ oz dwarf beans, trimmed and
halved in length
salt and pepper

1 Heat the oil in a large pan
and fry the onion and garlic
for 3–4 minutes or until soft. Add
the cubed potato and fry for a
further 2–3 minutes.

2 Stir in the stock, bring to
a boil and leave to simmer for
5 minutes.

3 Add the cucumber to the
pan and cook for a further
3 minutes or until the potatoes are
tender. Test by inserting the tip of
a knife into the potato cubes – it
should pass through easily.

4 Add the watercress and allow
to wilt. Then place the soup
in a food processor and blend until
smooth. Alternatively, before
adding the watercress, mash the
soup with a potato masher and
push through a strainer, then chop
the watercress finely and stir into
the soup.

5 Bring a small pan of water to a
boil and steam the beans for
3–4 minutes or until tender.

6 Add the beans to the soup,
season and warm through.

VARIATION

*Try using $4^1/_2$ oz snow peas instead
of the beans,
if you prefer.*

Tuscan Onion Soup

This soup is best made with white onions, which have a milder flavor than the more usual brown variety. If you cannot get hold of them, try using large Spanish onions instead.

Serves 4

INGREDIENTS

1³/₄ oz pancetta ham, diced
1 tbsp olive oil
4 large white onions, sliced thinly in rings
3 garlic cloves, chopped

3³/₄ cups hot chicken or ham stock
4 slices ciabatta or other Italian bread
3 tbsp butter
2³/₄ oz Gruyère or Cheddar

salt and pepper

1 Dry fry the pancetta in a large saucepan for 3–4 minutes until it begins to brown. Remove the pancetta from the pan and set aside until required.

2 Add the oil to the pan and cook the onions and garlic over a high heat for 4 minutes. Reduce the heat, cover and cook for 15 minutes until lightly caramelized.

3 Add the stock to the saucepan and bring to a boil. Reduce the heat and leave the mixture to simmer, covered, for about 10 minutes.

4 Toast the slices of ciabatta on both sides, under a preheated broiler, for 2–3 minutes or until golden. Spread the ciabatta with butter and top with the Gruyère or Cheddar cheese. Cut the bread into bite-size pieces.

5 Add the reserved pancetta to the soup and season to taste with salt and pepper. Pour into 4 soup bowls and top with the toasted bread.

COOK'S TIP

Pancetta is similar to bacon, but it is air- and salt-cured for about 6 months. Pancetta is available from most delicatessens and some large supermarkets. If you cannot obtain pancetta use unsmoked bacon instead.

Brown Lentil Soup with Pasta

In Italy, this soup is called Minestrade Lentiche. *A* minestra *is a soup cooked with pasta; in this case* farfalline, *a small bow-shaped variety, is used. Served with lentils, this hearty soup is a meal in itself.*

Serves 4

INGREDIENTS

4 rashers sliced bacon, cut into small squares
1 onion, chopped
2 garlic cloves, minced

2 celery stalks, chopped
$1/4$ cup farfalline or spaghetti broken into small pieces
1 x $14^1/_2$ oz can brown lentils, drained

5 cups hot ham or vegetable stock
2 tbsp chopped, fresh mint

1 Place the bacon in a large skillet together with the onions, garlic, and celery. Dry fry for 4–5 minutes, stirring, until the onion is tender and the bacon is just beginning to brown.

2 Add the farfalline or spaghetti pieces to the skillet and cook, stirring, for about 1 minute to coat the pasta in the oil.

3 Add the lentils and the stock and bring to a boil. Reduce the heat and leave to simmer for 12–15 minutes or until the pasta is tender.

4 Remove the skillet from the heat and stir in the chopped fresh mint.

5 Transfer the soup to warm soup bowls and serve immediately.

COOK'S TIP

If you prefer to use dried lentils, add the stock before the pasta and cook for 1–1$1/4$ hours until the lentils are tender. Add the pasta and cook for a further 12–15 minutes.

VARIATION

Any type of pasta can be used in this recipe, try fusilli, conchiglie, or rigatoni, if you prefer.

Orange, Thyme, & Pumpkin Soup

This thick, creamy soup has a wonderful, warming
golden color. It is flavored with orange and thyme.

Serves 4

INGREDIENTS

2 tbsp olive oil
2 medium onions, chopped
2 cloves garlic, chopped
2 lb pumpkin, peeled and cut into
  1 inch chunks

$6^{1}/_{4}$ cups boiling vegetable or
  chicken stock
finely grated rind and juice of
  1 orange

3 tbsp fresh thyme, stalks removed
$^{2}/_{3}$ cup milk
salt and pepper
crusty bread, to serve

1 Heat the olive oil in a large saucepan. Add the onions to the pan and cook for 3–4 minutes or until soft. Add the garlic and pumpkin and cook for a further 2 minutes, stirring well.

2 Add the boiling vegetable or chicken stock, orange rind, and juice and 2 tablespoons of the thyme to the pan. Leave to simmer, covered, for 20 minutes or until the pumpkin is tender.

3 Place the mixture in a food processor and blend until smooth. Alternatively, mash the mixture with a potato masher until smooth. Season to taste with salt and pepper.

4 Return the soup to the saucepan and add the milk. Reheat the soup for 3–4 minutes or until it is very hot but not boiling. Sprinkle with the remaining fresh thyme just before serving.

5 Divide the soup among 4 warm soup bowls and serve with lots of fresh crusty bread.

COOK'S TIP

Pumpkins are usually large vegetables. To make things a little easier, ask the greengrocer to cut a chunk off for you. Alternatively, make double the quantity and freeze the soup for up to 3 months.

Creamy Tomato Soup

This quick and easy creamy soup has a lovely fresh tomato flavor.

Serves 4

INGREDIENTS

3 tbsp butter
1 lb 9oz ripe tomatoes, preferably
  plum, roughly chopped

3¾ hot vegetable stock
⅔ cup milk or light cream
¼ cup ground almonds
1 tsp sugar

2 tbsp shredded basil leaves
salt and pepper

1 Melt the butter in a large saucepan. Add the tomatoes and cook for 5 minutes until the skins start to wrinkle. Season to taste with salt and pepper.

2 Add the stock to the pan, bring to a boil, cover, and simmer for 10 minutes.

3 Meanwhile, under a preheated broiler, lightly toast the ground almonds until they are golden-brown. This will take only 1-2 minutes, so watch them closely.

4 Remove the soup from the heat and place in a food processor and blend the mixture to form a smooth consistency. Alternatively, mash the soup with a potato masher.

5 Pass the soup through a strainer to remove any tomato skin or pips.

6 Place the soup in the pan and return to the heat. Stir in the milk or cream, ground, almonds and sugar. Warm the soup through and add the shredded basil just before serving.

7 Transfer the creamy tomato soup to warm soup bowls and serve hot.

VARIATION

Very fine bread crumbs can be used instead of the ground almonds, if you prefer. Toast them in the same way as the almonds and add with the milk or cream in step 6.

Vegetable Soup with Cannelini Beans

*This wonderful combination of beans, vegetables, and vermicelli is
made even richer by the addition of pesto and dried mushrooms.*

Serves 4

INGREDIENTS

1 small eggplant
2 large tomatoes
1 potato, peeled
1 carrot, peeled
1 leek
14$^{1}/_{2}$ oz can cannelini beans

3$^{3}/_{4}$ cups hot vegetable or chicken
  stock
2 tsp dried basil
$^{1}/_{2}$ oz dried porcini mushrooms,
  soaked for 10 minutes in enough
  warm water to cover

$^{1}/_{4}$ cup vermicelli
3 tbsp pesto (see page 312 or use
  shop bought)
freshly grated Parmesan cheese, to
  serve (optional)

1 Slice the eggplant into rings about $^{1}/_{2}$ inch thick, then cut each ring into 4.

2 Cut the tomatoes and potato into small dice. Cut the carrot into sticks, about 1 inch long and cut the leek into rings.

3 Place the cannelini beans and their liquid in a large saucepan. Add the eggplant, tomatoes, potatoes, carrot, and leek, stirring to mix.

4 Add the stock to the pan and bring to a boil. Reduce the heat and leave to simmer for 15 minutes.

5 Add the basil, dried mushrooms, their soaking liquid, and the vermicelli and simmer for 5 minutes or until all of the vegetables are tender.

6 Remove the pan from the heat and stir in the pesto.

7 Serve with freshly grated Parmesan cheese, if using.

COOK'S TIP

*Porcini are a
wild mushroom grown in southern
Italy. When dried and rehydrated
they have a very intense flavor, so
although they are expensive to buy
only a small amount are required to
add flavor to soups or risottos.*

Tuscan Bean & Vegetable Soup

This thick, satisfying blend of beans and diced vegetables in a rich red wine and tomato stock, based on an Italian favorite, makes an ideal simple supper.

Serves 4

INGREDIENTS

1 medium onion, chopped
1 garlic clove, finely chopped
2 celery stalks, sliced
1 large carrot, diced
14 oz can chopped tomatoes
$^2/_3$ cup Italian red wine
5 cups fresh vegetable stock

1 tsp dried oregano
15 oz can mixed beans
  and legumes
2 medium zucchini, diced
1 tbsp tomato paste
salt and pepper

TO SERVE:
pesto sauce (see page 312 or use
  shop-bought)
crusty bread

1 Place the prepared onion, garlic, celery, and carrot in a large saucepan. Stir in the tomatoes, red wine, vegetable stock, and oregano.

2 Bring the vegetable mixture to a boil, cover, and leave to simmer for 15 minutes. Stir the beans and zucchini into the mixture, and continue to cook, uncovered, for a further 5 minutes.

3 Add the tomato paste to the mixture and season well with salt and pepper to taste. Then heat through, stirring occasionally, for a further 2–3 minutes, but do not allow the mixture to boil again.

4 Ladle the soup into warm bowls and serve with a spoonful of pesto on each portion and accompanied with crusty bread.

VARIATION

For a more substantial soup, add 12 oz diced lean cooked chicken or turkey with the tomato paste in step 3.

Dal Soup

Dal is the name given to a delicious Indian lentil dish. This soup is a variation of the theme –
it is made with red lentils and spiced with curry powder.

Serves 4

INGREDIENTS

2 tbsp butter
2 garlic cloves, minced
1 onion, chopped
$1/2$ tsp turmeric
1 tsp garam masala
$1/4$ tsp chili powder
1 tsp ground cumin

2 lb canned, chopped tomatoes,
  drained
1 cup red lentils
2 tsp lemon juice
$2 1/2$ cups vegetable stock

$1 1/4$ cups coconut milk
salt and pepper
chopped cilantro and lemon slices, to
  garnish
naan bread, to serve

1 Melt the butter in a large saucepan and sauté the garlic and onion for 2–3 minutes, stirring. Add the spices and cook for a further 30 seconds.

2 Stir in the tomatoes, red lentils, lemon juice, vegetable stock, and coconut milk and bring to a boil.

3 Reduce the heat and simmer for 25–30 minutes until the lentils are tender and cooked.

4 Season to taste and spoon the soup into a warm tureen. Garnish and serve with warm naan bread.

COOK'S TIP

You can buy cans of coconut milk
from supermarkets and
delicatessens. It can also be made by
grating creamed coconut, which
comes in the form of a solid bar, and
mixing it with water.

COOK'S TIP

Add small quantities
of hot water to the pan whilst the
lentils are cooking if they begin to
absorb too much of the liquid.

Potato, Cabbage, & Chorizo Soup

*Chorizo is a spicy sausage originating from Spain where it is used to add
its unique strong flavor to enhance many traditional dishes.*

Serves 4

INGREDIENTS

2 tbsp olive oil
3 large potatoes, cubed
2 red onions, quartered
1 garlic clove, minced

$4^1/2$ cups pork or vegetable stock
$5^1/2$ oz Savoy cabbage, shredded

$1^3/4$ oz chorizo sausage, sliced
salt and pepper
paprika, to garnish

1 Heat the olive oil in a large saucepan and add the cubed potatoes, quartered red onions, and garlic. Sauté gently for 5 minutes, stirring constantly.

2 Add the pork or vegetable stock and bring to a boil. Reduce the heat and cover the saucepan. Simmer the vegetables for about 20 minutes until the potatoes are tender.

3 Process the soup in a food processor or blender in 2 batches for 1 minute each. Return the puréed soup to a clean pan.

4 Add the shredded Savoy cabbage and sliced chorizo sausage to the pan and cook for a further 7 minutes. Season to taste.

5 Ladle the soup into warmed soup bowls, garnish with a sprinkling of paprika and serve.

COOK'S TIP

Chorizo sausage requires no pre-cooking. In this recipe, it is added towards the end of the cooking time so that it does not to overpower the other flavors in the soup.

VARIATION

If chorizo sausage is not available, you could use any other spicy sausage or even salami in its place.

Celery, Stilton, & Walnut Soup

*This is a classic combination of ingredients all brought
together in a delicious, creamy soup.*

Serves 4

INGREDIENTS

4 tbsp butter
2 shallots, chopped
3 celery stalks, chopped
1 garlic clove, minced
2 tbsp all-purpose flour

$2^1/_2$ cups vegetable stock
$1^1/_4$ cups milk
$1^1/_2$ cups blue Stilton cheese,
 crumbled, plus extra to garnish
2 tbsp walnut halves,
 roughly chopped

$^2/_3$ cup unsweetened yogurt
salt and pepper
chopped celery leaves, to garnish

1 Melt the butter in a large saucepan and sauté the shallots, celery, and garlic for 2–3 minutes, stirring, until soft.

2 Add the flour and cook for 30 seconds.

3 Gradually stir in the vegetable stock and milk and bring to a boil.

4 Reduce the heat to a simmer and add the crumbled blue Stilton cheese and walnut halves.

Cover and simmer for 20 minutes.

5 Stir in the unsweetened yogurt and heat for a further 2 minutes without boiling.

6 Season the soup, then transfer to a warm soup tureen or individual serving bowls, garnish with chopped celery leaves and extra crumbled blue Stilton cheese and serve at once.

VARIATION

Use an alternative blue cheese, such as Dolcelatte or Gorgonzola, if preferred or a strong vegetarian Cheddar cheese, grated.

COOK'S TIP

As well as adding protein, vitamins, and useful fats to the diet, nuts add important flavor and texture to vegetarian meals.

Red bell Pepper & Chili Soup

This soup has a real Mediterranean flavor, using sweet red bell peppers, tomato, chili and basil. It is great served with a warm olive bread.

Serves 4

INGREDIENTS

8 oz red bell peppers,
   seeded and sliced
1 onion, sliced
2 garlic cloves, minced
1 green chili, chopped
1 1/2 cups sieved tomatoes

2 1/2 cups vegetable stock

2 tbsp chopped basil
fresh basil sprigs, to garnish

1 Put the bell peppers in a large saucepan with the onion, garlic, and chili. Add the sieved tomatoes and vegetable stock and bring to a boil, stirring well.

2 Reduce the heat to a simmer and cook for 20 minutes or until the bell peppers have softened. Drain, reserving the liquid and vegetables separately.

3 Strain the vegetables by pressing through a strainer with the back of a spoon. Alternatively, blend in a food processor until smooth.

4 Return the vegetable purée to a clean saucepan with the reserved cooking liquid. Add the basil and heat through until hot. Garnish the soup with fresh basil sprigs and serve.

COOK'S TIP

Basil is a useful herb to grow at home. It can be grown easily in a window box.

VARIATION

This soup is also delicious served cold with 2/3 cup of unsweetened yogurt swirled into it.

Indian Potato & Pea Soup

*A slightly hot and spicy Indian flavor is given to this soup with
the use of garam masala, chili, cumin, and cilantro.*

Serves 4

INGREDIENTS

2 tbsp vegetable oil
8 oz mealy potatoes, diced
1 large onion, chopped
2 garlic cloves, minced
1 tsp garam masala
1 tsp ground coriander

1 tsp ground cumin
3³/₄ cups vegetable stock
1 red chili, chopped

3¹/₂ oz frozen English peas
4 tbsp unsweetened yogurt

salt and pepper
chopped fresh cilantro, to garnish

1 Heat the vegetable oil in a large saucepan and add the diced potatoes, onion, and garlic. Sauté gently for about 5 minutes, stirring constantly.

2 Add the ground spices and cook for 1 minute, stirring all the time.

3 Stir in the vegetable stock and chopped red chili and bring the mixture to a boil. Reduce the heat, cover the pan and simmer for 20 minutes until the potatoes begin to break down.

4 Add the peas and cook for a further 5 minutes. Stir in the yogurt and season to taste.

5 Pour into warmed soup bowls, garnish with chopped fresh cilantro and serve hot with warm bread.

COOK'S TIP

Potatoes blend perfectly with spices, this soup being no exception. For an authentic Indian dish, serve this soup with warm naan bread.

VARIATION

For slightly less heat, seed the chili before adding it to the soup. Always wash your hands after handling chilies as they contain volatile oils that can irritate the skin and make your eyes burn if you touch your face.

Sweet Potato & Onion Soup

This simple recipe uses the sweet potato with its distinctive flavor and color as the base for a delicious soup with a hint of orange and cilantro.

Serves 4

INGREDIENTS

2 tbsp vegetable oil
2 lb sweet potatoes, diced
1 carrot, diced
2 onions, sliced
2 garlic cloves, minced

2¹/₂ cups vegetable stock
1¹/₄ cups unsweetened orange juice
1 cup unsweetened yogurt
2 tbsp chopped fresh cilantro

salt and pepper

TO GARNISH:
cilantro sprigs
orange rind

1 Heat the vegetable oil in a large saucepan and add the diced sweet potatoes and carrot, sliced onions, and garlic. Sauté gently for 5 minutes, stirring constantly.

2 Pour in the vegetable stock and orange juice and bring them to a boil.

3 Reduce the heat to a simmer, cover the saucepan and cook the vegetables for 20 minutes or until the sweet potato and carrot cubes are tender.

4 Transfer the mixture to a food processor or blender in batches and process for 1 minute until puréed. Return the purée to the rinsed-out saucepan.

5 Stir in the unsweetened yogurt and chopped cilantro and season to taste. Serve the soup garnished with cilantro sprigs and orange rind.

COOK'S TIP

This soup can be chilled before serving, if preferred. If chilling it, stir the yogurt into the dish just before serving. Serve in chilled bowls.

Broccoli & Potato Soup

*This creamy soup has a delightful pale green coloring and rich
flavor from the blend of tender broccoli and blue cheese.*

Serves 4

INGREDIENTS

2 tbsp olive oil
2 potatoes, diced
1 onion, diced
8 oz broccoli florets

$4^{1}/_{2}$ oz blue cheese, crumbled
$4^{1}/_{2}$ cups vegetable stock

$^{2}/_{3}$ cup heavy cream
pinch of paprika
salt and pepper

1 Heat the oil in a large saucepan and add the diced potatoes and onion. Sauté gently for 5 minutes, stirring constantly.

2 Reserve a few broccoli florets for the garnish and add the remaining broccoli to the pan. Add the cheese and stock.

3 Bring to a boil, then reduce the heat, cover the pan and simmer for 25 minutes until the potatoes are tender.

4 Transfer the soup to a food processor or blender in 2 batches and process until the mixture is a smooth purée.

5 Return the purée to a clean saucepan and stir in the cream and a pinch of paprika. Season to taste with salt and pepper.

6 Blanch the reserved broccoli florets in a little boiling water for about 2 minutes, then drain with a draining spoon.

7 Pour the soup into warmed bowls and garnish with the broccoli florets and a sprinkling of paprika. Serve immediately.

COOK'S TIP

*This soup freezes very successfully.
Follow the method described here
up to step 4, and freeze the soup
after it has been puréed. Add
the cream and paprika just before
serving. Garnish and serve.*

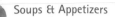

Chicken & Corn Soup

This heart-warming soup is both quick and easy to make.

Serves 4

INGREDIENTS

1 lb boned chicken breasts, cut into
strips
5 cups chicken stock
⁵/₈ cup heavy cream
³/₄ cup dried vermicelli

1 tbsp cornstarch
3 tbsp milk

6 oz corn kernels
salt and pepper

1 Put the chicken, stock, and cream into a large saucepan and bring to a boil over a low heat. Reduce the heat slightly and simmer for about 20 minutes. Season the soup with salt and black pepper to taste.

2 Meanwhile, cook the vermicelli in lightly salted boiling water for 10-12 minutes, until just tender. Drain the pasta and keep warm.

3 In a small bowl, mix together the cornstarch and milk to make a smooth paste. Stir the cornstarch into the soup until thickened.

4 Add the corn and vermicelli to the pan and heat through.

5 Transfer the soup to a warm tureen or individual soup bowls and serve immediately.

COOK'S TIP

If you are short of time, buy ready-cooked chicken, remove any skin and cut it into slices.

VARIATION

For crab and corn soup, substitute 1 lb cooked crabmeat for the chicken breasts. Flake the crabmeat well before adding it to the saucepan and reduce the cooking time by 10 minutes. For a Chinese-style soup, substitute egg noodles for the vermicelli and use canned, creamed corn.

Cream of Chicken Soup

Tarragon adds a delicate aniseed flavor to this tasty soup.
If you can't find tarragon, use parsley for a fresh taste.

Serves 4

INGREDIENTS

4 tbsp unsalted butter
1 large onion, peeled and chopped
10$^{1}/_{2}$ oz cooked chicken,
  shredded finely
2$^{1}/_{2}$ cups chicken stock
1 tbsp chopped fresh tarragon

$^{2}/_{3}$ cup heavy cream
salt and pepper
fresh tarragon leaves, to garnish
deep fried croutons, to serve

1 Melt the butter in a large saucepan and fry the onion for 3 minutes.

2 Add the chicken to the pan with 1$^{1}/_{4}$ cups of the chicken stock.

3 Bring to a boil and simmer for 20 minutes. Allow to cool, then liquidize the soup.

4 Add the remainder of the stock and season with salt and pepper.

5 Add the chopped tarragon, pour the soup into a tureen or individual serving bowls, and add a swirl of cream.

6 Garnish the soup with fresh tarragon and serve with deep fried croutons.

VARIATION

To make garlic croutons, mince 3–4 garlic cloves in a mortar and pestle and add to the oil.

VARIATION

If you can't find fresh tarragon, freeze-dried tarragon makes a good substitute. light cream can be used instead of the heavy cream.

Cream of Chicken & Tomato Soup

*This soup is very good made with fresh tomatoes,
but if you prefer, you can use canned tomatoes.*

Serves 2

INGREDIENTS

4 tbsp unsalted butter
1 large onion, chopped
1 lb chicken, shredded very finely
2¹/₂ cups chicken stock
6 medium tomatoes, chopped finely
pinch of baking soda

1 tbsp superfine sugar
²/₃ cup heavy cream
salt and pepper
fresh basil leaves, to garnish
croutons, to serve

1 Melt the butter in a large saucepan and fry the onion and shredded chicken for 5 minutes.

2 Add 1¼ cups chicken stock to the pan, with the tomatoes and bicarbonate of baking soda.

3 Bring the soup to a boil and simmer for 20 minutes.

4 Allow the soup to cool, then blend in a food processor.

5 Return the soup to the pan, add the remaining chicken stock, season, and add the sugar. Pour the soup into a tureen and add a swirl of heavy cream. Serve the soup with croutons and garnish with basil.

COOK'S TIP

*For a healthier version of this soup,
use light cream instead
of the heavy cream
and omit the sugar.*

VARIATION

*For an Italian-style soup, add
1 tbsp chopped fresh basil with the
stock in step 2. Alternatively, add
¹/₂ tsp curry powder or chili
powder to make a spicier
version of this soup.*

Beef & Vegetable Noodle Soup

Thin strips of beef are marinated in soy sauce and garlic to form the basis of this delicious soup. Served with noodles, it is both filling and delicious.

Serves 4

INGREDIENTS

8 oz lean beef	8 oz egg noodles	pinch of chili powder
1 garlic clove, minced	$3^3/_4$ cups beef stock	
2 scallions, chopped	3 baby-corn-on-the-cobs, sliced	
3 tbsp soy sauce	$^1/_2$ leek, shredded	
1 tsp sesame oil	$4^1/_2$ oz broccoli, cut into florets	

1 Using a sharp knife, cut the beef into thin strips and place them in a shallow glass bowl.

2 Add the garlic, scallions, soy sauce, and sesame oil and mix together well, turning the beef to coat. Cover and leave to marinate in the refrigerator for 30 minutes.

3 Cook the noodles in a saucepan of boiling water for 3–4 minutes. Drain the noodles thoroughly and set aside until required.

4 Put the beef stock in a large saucepan and bring to a boil.

5 Add the beef, together with the marinade, the corn, leek, and broccoli. Cover and leave to simmer over a low heat for 7–10 minutes, or until the beef and vegetables are tender and cooked through.

6 Stir in the noodles and chili powder and cook for a further 2–3 minutes. Transfer to bowls and serve immediately.

COOK'S TIP

Vary the vegetables used, or use those to hand. If preferred, use a few drops of chili sauce instead of chili powder, but remember it is very hot!

Lamb & Rice Soup

This is a very filling soup, as it contains rice and tender pieces of lamb.
Serve before a light main course.

Serves 4

INGREDIENTS

5¹/₂ oz lean lamb
¹/₄ cup rice
3³/₄ cups lamb stock
1 leek, sliced

1 garlic clove, thinly sliced
2 tsp light soy sauce
1 tsp rice-wine vinegar
1 medium open-cap mushroom,

salt

1 Using a sharp knife, trim any fat from the lamb and cut the meat into thin strips. Set aside until required.

2 Bring a large pan of lightly salted water to a boil and add the rice. Bring back to a boil, stir once, reduce the heat and cook for 10–15 minutes, until tender. Drain, rinse under cold running water, drain again, and set aside until required.

3 Meanwhile, put the lamb stock in a large saucepan and bring to a boil.

4 Add the lamb strips, leek, garlic, soy sauce, and rice-wine vinegar to the stock in the pan. Reduce the heat, cover and leave to simmer for 10 minutes, or until the lamb is tender and cooked through.

5 Add the mushroom slices and the rice to the pan and cook for a further 2–3 minutes, or until the mushroom is completely cooked through.

6 Ladle the soup into 4 individual warmed soup bowls and serve immediately.

COOK'S TIP

Use a few dried shiitake mushrooms, rehydrated according to the packet directions and chopped, as an alternative to the open-cap mushroom. Add the shiitake mushrooms with the lamb in step 4.

Chinese Potato & Pork Broth

In this recipe the pork is seasoned with traditional Chinese flavorings — soy sauce, rice-wine vinegar, and a dash of sesame oil.

Serves 4

INGREDIENTS

4¹/₂ cups chicken stock
2 large potatoes, diced
2 tbsp rice-wine vinegar
4¹/₂ oz pork tenderloin, sliced
2 tbsp cornstarch

4 tbsp water
1 tbsp light soy sauce
1 tsp sesame oil
1 carrot, cut into very thin strips
1 tsp gingerroot, chopped

3 scallions, sliced thinly
1 red bell pepper, sliced
8 oz can bamboo shoots, drained

1 Add the chicken stock, diced potatoes, and 1 tbsp of the rice-wine vinegar to a saucepan and bring to a boil. Reduce the heat until the stock is just simmering.

2 In a small bowl, mix the cornstarch with the water. Stir the mixture into the hot stock.

3 Bring the stock back to a boil, stirring until thickened, then reduce the heat until it is just simmering again.

4 Place the pork slices in a shallow dish and season with the remaining rice-wine vinegar, soy sauce and sesame oil.

5 Add the pork slices, carrot strips, and chopped ginger to the stock and cook for 10 minutes. Stir in the sliced scallions, red bell pepper, and bamboo shoots. Cook for a further 5 minutes.

6 Pour the soup into warmed bowls and serve immediately.

COOK'S TIP

Sesame oil is very strongly flavored and is, therefore, only used in small quantities.

VARIATION

For extra heat, add 1 chopped red chili or 1 tsp of chili powder to the soup in step 5.

Mussel & Potato Soup

This quick and easy soup would make a delicious summer lunch served with fresh crusty bread.

Serves 4

INGREDIENTS

1 lb 10 oz mussels
2 tbsp olive oil
7 tbsp unsalted butter
2 slices rindless fatty bacon, chopped
1 onion, chopped
2 garlic cloves, minced

$^{1}/_{2}$ cup all purpose flour
1 lb potatoes, thinly sliced
$^{3}/_{4}$ cup dried conchigliette
1$^{1}/_{4}$ cups heavy cream
1 tbsp lemon juice
2 egg yolks
salt and pepper

TO GARNISH:
2 tbsp finely chopped fresh parsley
lemon wedges

1 Debeard the mussels and scrub them under cold water for 5 minutes. Discard any mussels that do not close immediately when sharply tapped.

2 Bring a large pan of water to a boil, add the mussels, oil, and a little pepper and cook until the mussels open.

3 Drain the mussels, reserving the cooking liquid. Discard any mussels that are closed. Remove the mussels from their shells.

4 Melt the butter in a large saucepan, add the bacon, onion, and garlic and cook for 4 minutes. Carefully stir in the flour. Measure 5 cups of the reserved cooking liquid and stir it into the pan.

5 Add the potatoes to the pan and simmer for 5 minutes. Add the conchigliette and simmer for a further 10 minutes.

6 Add the cream and lemon juice, season to taste with salt and pepper, then add the mussels to the pan.

7 Blend the egg yolks with 1-2 tbsp of the remaining cooking liquid, stir into the pan and cook for 4 minutes.

8 Ladle the soup into 4 warm individual soup bowls, garnish with the chopped fresh parsley and lemon wedges and serve immediately.

Italian Fish Soup

This colorful mixed seafood soup would be
superbly complemented by a dry white wine.

Serves 4

INGREDIENTS

4 tbsp butter
1 lb assorted fish fillets, such as red
   mullet and snapper
1 lb prepared seafood, such as squid
   and shrimp
8 oz fresh crabmeat
1 large onion, sliced

$^1/_4$ cup all-purpose flour
5 cups fish stock
$^3/_4$ cup dried pasta shapes, such as
   ditalini or elbow macaroni
1 tbsp anchovy extract
grated rind and juice of 1 orange
$^1/_4$ cup dry sherry

1$^1/_4$ cups heavy cream
salt and black pepper
crusty brown bread, to serve

1 Melt the butter in a large
saucepan, add the fish fillets,
seafood, crabmeat, and onion and
cook gently over a low heat for
6 minutes.

2 Add the flour to the mixture,
stirring thoroughly to avoid
any lumps.

3 Gradually add the fish stock,
stirring constantly, until the
soup comes to a boil. Reduce the
heat and simmer for 30 minutes.

4 Add the pasta to the pan and
cook for a further 10 minutes.

5 Stir in the anchovy extract,
orange rind, orange juice,
sherry, and heavy cream. Season to
taste with salt and pepper.

6 Heat the soup until
completely warmed through.
Transfer the soup to a tureen or to
warm soup bowls and serve with
crusty brown bread.

COOK'S TIP

The heads, tails, trimmings, and
bones of virtually any non-oily fish
can be used to make fish stock.
Simmer 2 lb fish pieces in a large
saucepan with 5 fl oz white wine,
1 chopped onion, 1 sliced carrot, 1
sliced celery stalk, 4 black
peppercorns, 1 bouquet garni, and
7½ cups water for
30 minutes, then strain.

Coconut & Crab Soup

Thai red curry paste is quite fiery, but adds a superb flavor to this dish.
It is available in jars or packets from supermarkets.

Serves 4

INGREDIENTS

1 tbsp peanut oil

2 tbsp Thai red curry paste

1 red bell pepper, seeded and sliced

2¹/₂ cups coconut milk

2¹/₂ cups fish stock

2 tbsp fish sauce

8 oz canned or fresh white crabmeat

8 oz fresh or frozen crab claws

2 tbsp chopped fresh cilantro

3 scallions, trimmed and sliced

1 Heat the oil in a large preheated wok.

2 Add the red curry paste and red bell pepper to the wok and stir-fry for 1 minute.

3 Add the coconut milk, fish stock, and fish sauce to the wok and bring to a boil.

4 Add the crabmeat, crab claws, cilantro, and scallions to the wok. Stir the mixture well and heat thoroughly for 2–3 minutes.

5 Transfer the soup to warm bowls and serve hot.

COOK'S TIP

Clean the wok after each use by washing it with water, using a mild detergent if necessary, and a soft cloth or brush. Do not scrub or use any abrasive cleaner as this will scratch the surface. Dry thoroughly with paper towels or over a low heat, then wipe the surface all over with a little oil. This forms a sealing layer to protect the surface of the wok from moisture and prevents it rusting.

COOK'S TIP

Coconut milk adds a sweet and creamy flavor to the dish. It is available in powdered form or in tins ready to use.

Crab & Ginger Soup

*Two classic ingredients in Chinese cooking are blended together
in this recipe for a special soup.*

Serves 4

INGREDIENTS

1 carrot, chopped
1 leek, chopped
1 bay leaf
3³/₄ cups fish stock

2 medium-sized cooked crabs
1-inch piece fresh gingerroot, grated
1 tsp light soy sauce
¹/₂ tsp ground star anise

salt and pepper

1 Put the carrot, leek, bay leaf, and stock into a large pan and bring to a boil. Reduce the heat, cover, and leave to simmer for about 10 minutes, or until the vegetables are nearly tender.

2 Meanwhile, remove all of the meat from the cooked crabs. Break off the claws, break the joints, and remove the meat (you may require a fork or skewer for this). Add the crabmeat to the saucepan of fish stock.

3 Add the ginger, soy sauce, and star anise to the fish stock and bring to a boil. Leave to simmer for about 10 minutes, or until the vegetables are tender and the crab is heated through. Season to taste with salt and pepper.

4 Ladle the soup into warmed serving bowls and garnish with crab claws. Serve at once.

COOK'S TIP

*If fresh crabmeat is unavailable,
use drained canned
crabmeat or thawed frozen
crabmeat instead.*

COOK'S TIP

*To prepare cooked crab, loosen the
meat from the shell by banging the
back of the underside with a
clenched fist. Stand the crab on its
edge with the shell towards you.
Force the shell from the body with
your thumbs. Twist off the legs and
claws and remove the meat. Twist
off the tail and discard. Remove and
discard the gills from each side of the
body. Cut the body in half along
the center and remove all of the
meat. Scoop the brown meat from
the shell with a spoon.*

Chili Fish Soup

Shiitake mushrooms add an intense flavor to this soup which is unique.
Try to obtain them if you can, otherwise use opencap mushrooms, sliced.

Serves 4

INGREDIENTS

1/2 oz shiitake dried mushrooms

2 tbsp sunflower oil

1 onion, sliced

1 1/2 cups snow peas

1 1/2 cups bamboo shoots

3 tbsp sweet chili sauce

5 cups fish or vegetable stock

3 tbsp light soy sauce

2 tbsp fresh cilantro

1 lb cod fillet, skinned and cubed

1 Place the mushrooms in a large bowl. Pour over enough boiling water to cover and leave to stand for 5 minutes. Drain the mushrooms thoroughly. Using a sharp knife, roughly chop the mushrooms.

2 Heat the sunflower oil in a preheated wok. Add the onion to the wok and stir-fry for 5 minutes, or until softened.

3 Add the snow peas, bamboo shoots, chili sauce, stock, and soy sauce to the wok and bring to a boil.

4 Add the cilantro and cubed fish to the wok. Leave to simmer for 5 minutes or until the fish is cooked through.

5 Transfer the soup to warm bowls, garnish with extra cilantro if wished and serve hot.

COOK'S TIP

There are many different varieties of dried mushrooms, but shiitake are best. They are not cheap, but a small amount will go a long way.

VARIATION

Cod is used in this recipe as it is a meaty white fish. For real luxury, use angler fish tail instead.

Chinese Omelet

This is a fairly filling omelet, as it contains chicken and shrimp.
It is cooked as a whole omelet and then sliced for serving.

Serves 4

INGREDIENTS

8 eggs
2 cups cooked chicken, shredded
12 jumbo shrimp, peeled and

deveined
2 tbsp chopped chives
2 tsp light soy sauce

dash of chili sauce
2 tbsp vegetable oil

1 Lightly beat the eggs in a large mixing bowl.

2 Add the shredded chicken and jumbo shrimp to the eggs, mixing well.

3 Stir in the chopped chives, soy sauce, and chili sauce, mixing well.

4 Heat the oil in a large skillet over a medium heat and add the egg mixture, tilting the pan to coat the base completely. Cook over a medium heat, gently stirring the omelet with a fork, until the surface is just set and the underside is a golden brown color.

5 When the omelet is set, slide it out of the pan, with the aid of a spatula.

6 Cut the omelet into squares or slices to serve.

VARIATION

You could add extra flavor to the omelet by stirring in 3 tbsp finely chopped fresh cilantro or 1 tsp sesame seeds with the chives in step 3.

COOK'S TIP

Add English peas or other vegetables to the omelet and serve as a main course for 2 people.

Crispy Seaweed

This is a tasty Chinese starter or accompaniment which is not all that it seems. Pak choi is fried, salted and tossed with pine nuts, seaweed being totally absent from the recipe!

Serves 4

INGREDIENTS

2.4 lb pak choi
peanut oil, for deep frying
  (about 3³/₄ cups)

1 tsp salt
1 tbsp superfine sugar

2¹/₂ tbsp toasted pine nuts

1 Rinse the pak choi leaves under cold running water, then pat dry thoroughly with absorbent paper towels.

2 Roll each pak choi leaf up, then slice through thinly so that the leaves are finely shredded.

3 Heat the oil in a large wok. Carefully add the shredded leaves and fry for about 30 seconds or until they shrivel up and become crispy (you may need to do this in about 4 batches).

4 Remove the crispy seaweed from the wok with a draining spoon and drain on absorbent paper towels.

5 Transfer the crispy seaweed to a large bowl and toss with the salt, sugar, and pine nuts. Serve immediately.

COOK'S TIP

As a time-saver you can use a food processor to shred the pak choi finely. Make sure you use only the best leaves; sort through the pak choi and discard any tough, outer leaves as these will spoil the overall taste and texture of the dish.

VARIATION

Use savoy cabbage instead of the pak choi if it is unavailable, making sure the leaves are well dried before frying.

Hummus & Garlic Toasts

Hummus is a real favorite spread on these garlic toasts for a delicious starter or as part of a light lunch.

Serves 4

INGREDIENTS

HUMMUS:
14 oz can garbanzo beans
juice of 1 large lemon
6 tbsp sesame seed paste
2 tbsp olive oil
2 garlic cloves, minced

salt and pepper
chopped fresh cilantro and black
   olives, to garnish

TOASTS:
1 ciabatta loaf, sliced
2 garlic cloves, minced
1 tbsp chopped fresh cilantro
4 tbsp olive oil

1 To make the hummus, firstly drain the garbanzo beans, reserving a little of the liquid. Put the garbanzo beans and liquid in a food processor and blend, gradually adding the reserved liquid and lemon juice. Blend well after each addition until smooth.

2 Stir in the sesame seed paste and all but 1 teaspoon of the olive oil. Add the garlic, season to taste, and blend again until smooth.

3 Spoon the hummus into a serving dish. Drizzle the remaining olive oil over the top, garnish with chopped cilantro and olives. Leave to chill in the refrigerator while preparing the toasts.

4 Lay the slices of ciabatta on a broiler rack in a single layer.

5 Mix the garlic, cilantro and olive oil together and drizzle over the bread slices. Cook under a hot broiler for 2–3 minutes until

golden brown, turning once. Serve hot with the hummus.

COOK'S TIP

Make the hummus 1 day in advance, and chill, covered, in the refrigerator until required. Garnish and serve.

Mixed Bean Pâté

This is a really quick starter to prepare if canned beans are used.
Choose a wide variety of beans for color and flavor or use a can of mixed beans.

Serves 4

INGREDIENTS

14 oz can mixed beans, drained
2 tbsp olive oil
juice of 1 lemon
2 garlic cloves, minced

1 tbsp chopped fresh cilantro
2 scallions, chopped
salt and pepper

shredded scallions, to garnish

1 Rinse the beans thoroughly under cold running water and drain well.

2 Transfer the beans to a food processor or blender and process until smooth. Alternatively, place the beans in a bowl and mash with a fork or potato masher.

3 Add the olive oil, lemon juice, garlic, cilantro, and scallions and blend until fairly smooth. Season with salt and pepper to taste.

4 Transfer the pâté to a serving bowl and chill for at least 30 minutes. Garnish with shredded scallions and serve.

COOK'S TIP

Use canned beans which have no salt or sugar added and always rinse thoroughly before use.

COOK'S TIP

Serve the pâté with warm pocket bread or granary toast.

Paprika Crisps

These wafer-thin potato crisps are great cooked over a barbecue and served with spicy chicken or pork.
They also work well broiled, but they do not take on the 'smokey' flavor.

Serves 4

INGREDIENTS

2 large potatoes   ¹/₂ tsp paprika pepper   salt
3 tbsp olive oil

1 Using a sharp knife, slice the potatoes very thinly so that they are almost transparent. Drain the potato slices thoroughly and pat dry with paper towels.

2 Heat the oil in a large skillet and add the paprika, stirring constantly, to ensure that the paprika doesn't catch and burn.

3 Add the potato slices to the skillet and cook them in a single layer for about 5 minutes or until the potato slices just begin to curl slightly at the edges.

4 Remove the potato slices from the pan using a perforated spoon and transfer them to paper towels to drain thoroughly.

5 Thread the potato slices on to several wooden kabob skewers.

6 Sprinkle the potato slices with a little salt and cook over a medium hot barbecue or under a medium broiler for 10 minutes, turning frequently, until the potato slices begin to crispen. Sprinkle with a little more salt, if preferred, and serve.

VARIATION

You could use curry powder or any other spice to flavor the crisps instead of the paprika, if you prefer.

Carrot, Fennel, & Potato Medley

This is a colorful dish of shredded vegetables in a fresh garlic and honey dressing.
It is delicious served with crusty bread to mop up the dressing.

Serves 4

INGREDIENTS

2 tbsp olive oil
1 potato, cut into thin strips
1 fennel bulb, cut into thin strips
2 carrots, grated
1 red onion, cut into thin strips
chopped chives and fennel fronds, to
   garnish

DRESSING:
3 tbsp olive oil
1 tbsp garlic-wine vinegar
1 garlic clove, minced
1 tsp Dijon mustard
2 tsp clear honey
salt and pepper

1 Heat the olive oil in a skillet, add the potato and fennel slices and cook for 2–3 minutes until beginning to brown. Remove from the skillet with a draining spoon and drain on paper towels.

2 Arrange the carrot, red onion, potato, and fennel in separate piles on a serving plate.

3 Mix the dressing ingredients together and pour over the vegetables. Toss well and sprinkle with chopped chives and fennel fronds. Serve immediately or leave in the refrigerator until required.

VARIATION

Use mixed, grilled bell peppers or shredded leeks in this dish for variety, or add bean sprouts and a segmented orange, if you prefer.

COOK'S TIP

Fennel is an aromatic plant which has a delicate, aniseed flavor. It can be eaten raw in salads, or boiled, braised, sautéed or broiled. For this salad, if leek is unavailable, substitute 12 oz sliced leeks.

Seven Spice Eggplant

*This is a really simple dish which is perfect
served with a chili dip.*

Serves 4

INGREDIENTS

1 lb eggplant, wiped
1 egg white
3¹/₂ tbsp cornstarch

1 tsp salt
1 tbsp Thai seven spice seasoning
oil, for deep-frying

1 Using a sharp knife, slice the eggplant into thin rings.

2 Place the egg white in a small bowl and whip until light and foamy.

3 Mix together the cornflour, salt, and seven spice powder on a large plate.

4 Heat the oil for deep-frying in a large wok.

5 Dip each piece of eggplant into the beaten egg white then coat in the cornflour and seven spice mixture.

6 Deep-fry the eggplant slices, in batches, for 5 minutes, or until pale golden and crispy.

7 Transfer the eggplant to absorbent paper towels and leave to drain. Transfer to serving plates and serve hot.

COOK'S TIP

*Thai seven spice seasoning can be
found in the spice racks of most
large supermarkets.*

COOK'S TIP

*The best oil to use for deep-frying is
peanut oil which has a high smoke
point and mild flavor, so it will
neither burn or taint the food. About
1 pint oil is sufficient.*

Chicken Pan Bagna

Perfect for a picnic or packed lunch, this Mediterranean-style sandwich can be prepared in advance.

Serves 6

INGREDIENTS

1 large French stick
1 garlic clove
$^1/_2$ cup olive oil
$^3/_4$ oz canned anchovy fillets

2 oz cold roast chicken
2 large tomatoes, sliced
8 large, pitted black olives, chopped
pepper

1 Using a sharp bread knife, cut the French stick in half lengthways and open out.

2 Cut the garlic clove in half and rub over the bread.

3 Sprinkle the cut surface of the bread with the olive oil.

4 Drain the anchovies and set aside.

5 Thinly slice the chicken and arrange on top of the bread. Arrange the tomatoes and drained anchovies on top of the chicken.

6 Scatter with the chopped black olives and plenty of black pepper. Sandwich the loaf back together and wrap tightly in foil until required. Cut into slices to serve.

VARIATION

You could use Italian ciabatta or olive-studded focaccia bread instead of the French stick, if you prefer. The last few years have seen a veritable interest in different breads and supermarkets now stock a wide range from home and abroad.

COOK'S TIP

Arrange a few fresh basil leaves in between the tomato slices to add a warm, spicy flavor. Use a good quality olive oil in this recipe for extra flavor.

Tuscan Chicken Livers on Toast

Crostini are small pieces of toast with a savory topping.
In Italy this is a popular antipasto dish.

Serves 4

INGREDIENTS

2 tbsp olive oil
1 garlic clove, finely chopped
8 oz fresh or frozen chicken livers

4 fresh sage leaves, finely chopped or
  1 tsp dried, crumbled sage
2 tbsp white wine
2 tbsp lemon juice

salt and pepper
4 slices ciabatta or other Italian
  bread
wedges of lemon, to garnish

1 Heat the olive oil in a skillet and cook the garlic for 1 minute.

2 Rinse and roughly chop the chicken livers, using a sharp knife.

3 Add the chicken liver to the skillet together with the white wine and lemon juice. Cook for 3–4 minutes or until the juices from the chicken liver run clear.

4 Stir in the sage and season to taste with salt and pepper.

5 Under a preheated broiler, toast the bread for 2 minutes on both sides or until golden-brown.

6 Spoon the hot chicken livers on top of the toasted bread and serve garnished with a wedge of lemon.

COOK'S TIP

Overcooked liver is dry and tasteless. Cook the chopped liver for only 3–4 minutes – it should be soft and tender.

VARIATION

Another way to make crostini is to slice a crusty loaf or a French loaf into small rounds or squares. Heat the olive oil in a skillet and fry the slices of bread until golden brown and crisp on both sides. Remove the crostini from the pan with a draining spoon and leave to drain on paper towels. Top with the chicken livers.

Cured Meats with Olives & Tomatoes

This is a typical antipasto dish with the cold cured meats, stuffed olives, and fresh tomatoes, basil, and balsamic vinegar.

Serves 4

INGREDIENTS

4 plum tomatoes
1 tbsp balsamic vinegar
6 canned anchovy fillets, drained and rinsed

2 tbsp capers, drained and rinsed
4¹/₂ oz green olives, pitted
6 oz mixed, cured meats, sliced
8 fresh basil leaves

1 tbsp extra virgin olive oil
salt and pepper
crusty bread, to serve

1 Using a sharp knife, cut the tomatoes into evenly-sized slices. Sprinkle the tomato slices with the balsamic vinegar and a little salt and pepper to taste and set aside.

2 Chop the anchovy fillets into pieces measuring about the same length as the olives.

3 Push a piece of anchovy and a caper into each olive.

4 Arrange the sliced meat on 4 individual serving plates together with the tomatoes, filled olives, and basil leaves.

5 Drizzle the olive oil over the sliced meat, tomatoes, and olives.

6 Serve the cured meats, olives, and tomatoes with lots of fresh crusty bread.

COOK'S TIP

The cured meats for this recipe are up to your individual taste. They can include a selection of prosciutto, pancetta, bresaola (dried salt beef), and salame di Milano (pork and beef sausage).

COOK'S TIP

Fill a screw-top jar with the stuffed olives, cover with olive oil, and use when required – they will keep for 1 month in the refrigerator.

Fresh Figs with Prosciutto

This colorful fresh salad is delicious at any time of the year.

Serves 4

INGREDIENTS

1¹/₂ oz arugula
4 fresh figs
4 slices prosciutto

4 tbsp olive oil
1 tbsp fresh orange juice

1 tbsp clear honey
1 small red chili

1 Tear the arugula into more manageable pieces and arrange on 4 serving plates.

2 Using a sharp knife, cut each of the figs into quarters and place them on top of the arugula leaves.

3 Using a sharp knife, cut the prosciutto into strips and scatter over the arugula and figs.

4 Place the oil, orange juice, and honey in a screw-top jar. Shake the jar until the mixture emulsifies and forms a thick dressing. Transfer to a bowl.

5 Using a sharp knife, dice the chili, remembering not to touch your face before you have washed your hands (see Cook's Tip, right). Add the chopped chili to the dressing and mix well.

6 Drizzle the dressing over the prosciutto, arugula, and figs, tossing to mix well. Serve at once.

COOK'S TIP

Chilies can burn the skin for several hours after chopping, so it is advisable to wear gloves when you are handling the very hot varieties.

COOK'S TIP

Parma, in the Emilia-Romagna region of Italy, is famous for its ham, prosciutto di Parma, said to be the best in the world.

Shrimp Omelet

This is called Foo Yung *in China and is a classic dish which may be flavored with any ingredients you have to hand. It is a quick and delicious omelet.*

Serves 4

INGREDIENTS

3 tbsp sunflower oil
2 leeks, trimmed and sliced
12 oz raw jumbo shrimp
4 tbsp cornstarch

1 tsp salt
6 oz mushrooms, sliced
1 1/2 cups mung beansprouts
6 eggs

deep-fried leeks, to garnish (optional)

1 Heat the sunflower oil in a preheated wok. Add the leeks and stir-fry for 3 minutes.

2 Rinse the shrimp under cold running water and then pat dry with absorbent paper towels.

3 Mix together the cornstarch and salt in a large bowl.

4 Add the shrimp to the cornstarch and salt mixture and toss to coat all over.

5 Add the shrimp to the wok and stir-fry until the shrimp are almost cooked through.

6 Add the mushrooms and beansprouts to the wok and stir-fry for a further 2 minutes.

7 Beat the eggs with 3 tablespoons of cold water. Pour the egg mixture into the wok and cook until the egg sets, carefully turning over once. Turn the omelet out on to a clean board, divide into 4 and serve hot, garnished with deep-fried leeks (if using).

COOK'S TIP

If liked, divide the mixture into 4 once the initial cooking has taken place in step 6 and cook 4 individual omelets.

Salt & Pepper Shrimp

Szechuan peppercorns are very hot, adding heat and a red color to the shrimp.
They are effectively offset by the sugar in this recipe.

Serves 4

INGREDIENTS

2 tsp salt

1 tsp black pepper

2 tsp Szechuan peppercorns

1 tsp sugar

1 lb peeled raw jumbo shrimp

2 tbsp peanut oil

1 red chili, seeded and finely chopped

1 tsp freshly grated ginger

3 cloves garlic, minced

scallions, sliced, to garnish

shrimp crackers, to serve

1 Grind the salt, black pepper and Szechuan peppercorns in a mortar and pestle. Mix the salt and pepper mixture with the sugar and set aside until required.

2 Rinse the shrimp under cold running water and pat dry with absorbent paper towels.

3 Heat the oil in a preheated wok. Add the shrimp, chili, ginger, and garlic and stir-fry for 4–5 minutes, or until the shrimp are cooked through.

4 Add the salt and pepper mixture to the wok and stir-fry for 1 minute.

5 Transfer to warm serving bowls and garnish with the scallions. Serve hot with shrimp crackers.

COOK'S TIP

Szechuan peppercorns are also known as farchiew. *These wild reddish-brown peppercorns from the Szechuan region of China add an aromatic flavor to a dish.*

COOK'S TIP

Jumbo shrimps are widely available and are not only colorful and tasty, but they have a meaty texture, too. If cooked jumbo shrimp are used, add them with the salt and pepper mixture in step 4 – if the cooked shrimp are added any earlier they will toughen up and be inedible.

Sesame Shrimp Toasts

These small toasts are easy to prepare and are one of the most popular Chinese appetizers in the West. Make sure you serve plenty of them as they are very tasty!

Serves 4

INGREDIENTS

8 oz cooked, peeled
  shrimp
1 scallion
$^1/_4$ tsp salt

1 tsp light soy sauce
1 tbsp cornstarch
1 egg white, beaten

3 thin slices white bread,
  crusts removed
4 tbsp sesame seeds
vegetable oil, for deep-frying

1 Put the shrimp and scallion in a food processor and process until finely ground. Alternatively, chop them very finely. Transfer to a bowl and stir in the salt, soy sauce, cornstarch and egg white.

2 Spread the mixture on to one side of each slice of bread. Spread the sesame seeds on top of the mixture, pressing down well.

3 Cut each slice into four equal triangles or strips.

4 Heat the oil for deep-frying in a wok until almost smoking. Carefully place the triangles in the oil, coated side down, and cook for 2–3 minutes, until golden brown. Remove with a draining spoon and drain on paper towels. Serve hot.

VARIATION

If wished, you could add ½ tsp very finely chopped fresh gingerroot and 1 tsp Chinese rice wine to the shrimp mixture at the end of step 1.

COOK'S TIP

Fry the triangles in two batches, keeping the first batch warm while you cook the second, to prevent them from sticking together and overcooking.

Deep-Fried Seafood

Deep-fried seafood is popular all around the Mediterranean, where fish of all kinds is fresh and abundant. Serve with garlic mayonnaise and lemon wedges.

Serves 4

INGREDIENTS

7 oz prepared squid
7 oz raw jumbo shrimp, peeled
5^1/$_2$ oz whitebait
oil, for deep-frying

1^1/$_2$ oz all-purpose flour
1 tsp dried basil
salt and pepper

TO SERVE:
garlic mayonnaise (see Cook's Tip)
lemon wedges

1 Carefully rinse the squid, shrimp, and whitebait under cold running water, completely removing any dirt or grit.

2 Using a sharp knife, slice the squid into rings, leaving the tentacles whole.

3 Heat the oil in a large saucepan to 350°–375°F or until a cube of bread browns in 30 seconds.

4 Place the flour in a bowl and season with the salt, pepper, and basil.

5 Roll the squid, shrimp, and whitebait in the seasoned flour until coated all over. Carefully shake off any excess flour.

6 Cook the seafood in the heated oil in batches for 2–3 minutes or until crispy and golden all over. Remove all of the seafood with a draining spoon and leave to drain thoroughly on paper towels.

7 Transfer the deep-fried seafood to serving plates and serve with garlic mayonnaise (see Cook's Tip) and lemon wedges.

COOK'S TIP

To make garlic mayonnaise for serving with the deep-fried seafood, crush 2 garlic cloves, stir into 8 tablespoons of mayonnaise and season with salt and pepper and a little chopped parsley.

Snacks & Salads

Too frequently, leaf vegetables are overcooked and limp, with all the goodness and flavor boiled out, while salads are often nothing more than a dismal leaf or two of pale green lettuce with a slice of tomato and a dry ring of onion. Make the most of the wonderful range of fresh produce that is available in our shops and markets.

Steam broccoli and cabbage so that they are colorful and crunchy. Enjoy the wonderfully appetizing shades of orange and yellow bell peppers and the almost unbelievable purple-brown of eggplant. Try grating root vegetables – carrots and daikon – to add flavor and texture to garnishes and casseroles. Look out for red and curly lettuces to bring excitement to an enticing summer salad. Use sweet baby tomatoes in salads and on skewers, and raid your garden and windowsill for sprigs of fresh mint and basil leaves.

Nuts and seeds are high in fat, so both should be used in moderation. However, they are a valuable source of protein and minerals, and vegetarians and vegans in particular need to ensure that their diets contain these valuable ingredients.

Bean Curd & Vegetable Stir-Fry

*This is a quick dish to prepare, making it ideal as a mid-week supper dish,
after a busy day at work!*

Serves 4

INGREDIENTS

1¼ cups potatoes, cubed
1 tbsp olive oil
1 red onion, sliced
8 oz firm bean curd, diced
2 zucchini, diced
8 canned artichoke hearts, halved

⅔ cup sieved tomatoes
1 tsp superfine sugar

2 tbsp chopped basil
salt and pepper

1 Cook the potatoes in a saucepan of boiling water for 10 minutes. Drain thoroughly and set aside until required.

2 Heat the oil in a large skillet and sauté the red onion for 2 minutes until the onion has softened, stirring.

3 Stir in the bean curd and zucchini and cook for 3–4 minutes until they begin to brown slightly. Add the potatoes, stirring to mix.

4 Stir in the artichoke hearts, sieved tomatoes, sugar, and basil, season with salt and pepper and cook for a further 5 minutes, stirring well. Transfer the stir-fry to serving dishes and serve immediately.

VARIATION

Eggplants could be used instead of the zucchini, if preferred.

COOK'S TIP

Canned artichoke hearts should be drained thoroughly and rinsed before use because they often have salt added.

Scrambled Bean Curd on Toast

This is a delicious dish which would also serve as a light lunch or supper.

Serves 4

INGREDIENTS

6 tbsp vegetarian margarine
1 lb marinated, firm bean curd
1 red onion, chopped
1 red bell pepper, chopped

4 ciabatta rolls
2 tbsp chopped mixed herbs
salt and pepper
fresh herbs, to garnish

1 Melt the margarine in a skillet and crumble the bean curd into the pan.

2 Add the onion and bell pepper and cook for 3–4 minutes, stirring occasionally.

3 Meanwhile, slice the ciabatta rolls in half and toast under a hot broiler for about 2–3 minutes, turning once. Remove the toasts and transfer to a serving plate.

4 Add the herbs to the bean curd mixture, combine, and season.

5 Spoon the bean curd mixture on to the toast and garnish with fresh herbs. Serve at once.

COOK'S TIP

Marinated bean curd adds extra flavor to this dish. Smoked bean curd could be used in its place.

COOK'S TIP

Rub the cut surface of a garlic clove over the toasted ciabatta rolls for extra flavor.

Tagliatelle with Zucchini Sauce

*This is a really fresh tasting dish which is ideal with
a crisp white wine and some crusty bread.*

Serves 4

INGREDIENTS

1 lb 7 oz zucchini
6 tbsp olive oil
3 garlic cloves, minced
3 tbsp chopped basil
2 red chilies, sliced

juice of 1 large lemon
5 tbsp light cream
4 tbsp grated Parmesan cheese
8 oz tagliatelle
salt and pepper

1 Using a vegetable peeler, slice the zucchini into ribbons.

2 Heat the oil in a skillet and sauté the garlic for 30 seconds.

3 Add the zucchini and cook over a gentle heat, stirring, for 5–7 minutes.

4 Stir in the basil, chilies, lemon juice, light cream, and grated Parmesan cheese and season with salt and pepper to taste.

5 Meanwhile, cook the tagliatelle in a large pan of lightly salted boiling water for 10 minutes until 'al dente'. Drain the pasta thoroughly and put in a warm serving bowl.

6 Pile the zucchini mixture on top of the pasta. Serve immediately.

VARIATION

*Lime juice and
zest could be used instead of the
lemon as an alternative.*

Marinated Broiled Fennel

Fennel has a wonderful aniseed flavor which is ideal for broiling or grilling. Marinated in lime, garlic, oil, and mustard, this recipe is really delicious.

Serves 4

INGREDIENTS

2 fennel bulbs
1 red bell pepper, cut into large cubes
1 lime, cut into eight wedges

MARINADE:
2 tbsp lime juice
4 tbsp olive oil
2 garlic cloves, minced
1 tsp whole-grain mustard
1 tbsp chopped thyme

fennel fronds, to garnish
crisp salad, to serve

1 Cut each of the fennel bulbs into eight pieces and place in a shallow dish. Mix in the bell peppers.

2 To make the marinade, combine the lime juice, oil, garlic, mustard, and thyme. Pour the marinade over the fennel and bell peppers and leave to marinate for 1 hour.

3 Thread the fennel and bell peppers on to wooden skewers with the lime wedges.

Preheat a broiler to medium and broil the kabobs for 10 minutes, turning and basting with the marinade.

4 Transfer to serving plates, garnish with fennel fronds and serve with a crisp salad.

VARIATION

Substitute 2 tbsp orange juice for the lime juice and add 1 tbsp honey, if you prefer.

COOK'S TIP

Soak the skewers in water for 20 minutes before using to prevent them from burning during cooking.

Spinach & Pine Nut Pasta

Use any pasta shapes that you have for this recipe,
the tricolore pasta being visually the best to use.

Serves 4

INGREDIENTS

8 oz pasta shapes or spaghetti
1/2 cup olive oil
2 garlic cloves, minced
1 onion, quartered and sliced
3 large flat mushrooms, sliced

8 oz spinach
2 tbsp pine nuts
6 tbsp dry white wine
salt and pepper
Parmesan shavings, to garnish

1 Cook the pasta in a saucepan of boiling salted water for 8–10 minutes or until 'al dente'. Drain well.

2 Meanwhile, heat the oil in a large saucepan and sauté the garlic and onion for 1 minute.

3 Add the sliced mushrooms and cook for 2 minutes, stirring occasionally.

4 Add the spinach and cook for 4–5 minutes or until the spinach has wilted.

5 Stir in the pine nuts and wine, season well, and cook for 1 minute.

6 Transfer the pasta to a warm serving bowl and toss the sauce into it, mixing well. Garnish with shavings of Parmesan cheese and serve.

COOK'S TIP

'Al dente' means that the pasta
should be tender but still
have a bite to it.

COOK'S TIP

Freshly grate a little nutmeg over
the dish for extra flavor as it is
particularly good
with spinach.

Olive, bell Pepper, & Cherry Tomato Pasta

The sweet cherry tomatoes in this recipe add color and flavor and are complemented by the black olives and bell peppers.

Serves 4

INGREDIENTS

2 cups penne

2 tbsp olive oil

2 tbsp butter

2 garlic cloves, minced

1 green bell pepper, thinly sliced

1 yellow bell pepper, thinly sliced

16 cherry tomatoes, halved

1 tbsp chopped oregano

$^1/_2$ cup dry white wine

2 tbsp quartered, pitted black olives

$2^3/_4$ oz arugula

salt and pepper

fresh oregano sprigs, to garnish

1 Cook the pasta in a saucepan of boiling salted water for 8–10 minutes or until 'al dente'. Drain thoroughly.

2 Heat the oil and butter in a pan until the butter melts. Sauté the garlic for 30 seconds. Add the bell peppers and cook for 3–4 minutes, stirring.

3 Stir in the cherry tomatoes, oregano, wine, and olives and cook for 3–4 minutes. Season well with salt and pepper and stir in the arugula until just wilted.

4 Transfer the pasta to a serving dish, spoon over the sauce, and mix well. Garnish and serve.

VARIATION

If arugula is unavailable, spinach makes a good substitute. Follow the same cooking directions as for arugula.

COOK'S TIP

Ensure that the saucepan is large enough to prevent the pasta from sticking together during cooking.

Potato, bell Pepper, & Mushroom Hash

This is a quick one-pan dish which is ideal for a quick snack. Packed with color and flavor it is very versatile and you can add any other vegetable you have at hand.

Serves 4

INGREDIENTS

1¹/₂ lb potatoes, cubed
1 tbsp olive oil
2 garlic cloves, minced
1 green bell pepper, cubed
1 yellow bell pepper, cubed

3 tomatoes, diced
1 cup button mushrooms, halved
1 tbsp vegetarian Worcester sauce
2 tbsp chopped basil
salt and pepper

fresh basil sprigs, to garnish
warm, crusty bread, to serve

1 Cook the potatoes in a saucepan of boiling salted water for 7–8 minutes. Drain well and reserve.

2 Heat the oil in a large, heavy-bottomed skillet and cook the potatoes for 8–10 minutes, stirring until browned.

3 Add the garlic and bell peppers and cook for 2–3 minutes.

4 Stir in the tomatoes and mushrooms and cook, stirring, for 5–6 minutes.

5 Stir in the vegetarian Worcester sauce and basil and season well. Garnish and serve with crusty bread.

VARIATION

This dish can also be eaten cold as a salad.

COOK'S TIP

Most brands of Worcester sauce contain anchovies so make sure you choose a vegetarian variety.

Mixed Bean Pan-Fry

*Fresh green beans have a wonderful flavor that is hard to beat.
If you cannot find fresh beans, use thawed, frozen beans instead.*

Serves 4

INGREDIENTS

4 cups mixed green beans, such as
    fava beans or dwarf beans
2 tbsp vegetable oil
2 garlic cloves, minced
1 red onion, halved and sliced
8 oz firm marinated bean curd, diced

1 tbsp lemon juice
1/2 tsp turmeric
1 tsp ground mixed spice

2/3 cup vegetable stock
2 tsp sesame seeds

1 Trim and chop the green beans and set aside until required.

2 Heat the oil in a skillet and sauté the garlic and onion for 2 minutes, stirring well.

3 Add the bean curd and cook for 2–3 minutes until just beginning to brown.

4 Add the green beans and fava beans. Stir in the lemon juice, turmeric, mixed spice, and vegetable stock and bring to a boil.

5 Reduce the heat and simmer for 5–7 minutes or until the beans are tender. Sprinkle with sesame seeds and serve immediately.

VARIATION

Add lime juice instead of lemon, for an alternative citrus flavor.

VARIATION

Use smoked bean curd instead of marinated bean curd for an alternative flavor.

Garlic Mushrooms on Toast

This is so simple to prepare and looks great if you use a variety of mushrooms for shape and texture. Cooked in garlic butter, they are simply irresistible.

Serves 4

INGREDIENTS

6 tbsp vegetarian margarine
2 garlic cloves, minced

4 cups mixed mushrooms, such as
  open-cap, button, oyster, and
  shiitake, sliced
8 slices French bread
1 tbsp chopped parsley

salt and pepper

1 Melt the margarine in a skillet. Add the minced garlic and cook for 30 seconds, stirring.

2 Add the mushrooms and cook for 5 minutes, turning occasionally.

3 Toast the French bread slices under a preheated medium broiler for 2–3 minutes, turning once.

4 Transfer the toasts to a serving plate.

5 Toss the parsley into the mushrooms, mixing well, and season well with salt and pepper to taste.

6 Spoon the mushroom mixture over the bread and serve immediately.

COOK'S TIP

Add seasonings, such as curry powder or chili powder, to the mushrooms for extra flavor, if liked.

COOK'S TIP

Store mushrooms for 24–36 hours in the refrigerator, in paper bags, as they sweat in plastic. Wild mushrooms should be washed but other varieties can simply be wiped with a paper towel.

Refried Beans with Tortillas

Refried beans are a classic Mexican dish and are usually served as an accompaniment.
They are, however, delicious when served with warm tortillas and a quick onion relish.

Serves 4

INGREDIENTS

BEANS:
2 tbsp olive oil
1 onion, finely chopped
3 garlic cloves, minced
1 green chili, chopped
14 oz can red kidney beans, drained
14 oz can pinto beans, drained
2 tbsp chopped cilantro

$^2/_3$ cup vegetable stock
8 wheat tortillas
$^1/_4$ cup vegetarian Cheddar
   cheese, grated
salt and pepper

RELISH:
4 scallion, chopped

1 red onion, chopped
1 green chili, chopped
1 tbsp garlic-wine vinegar
1 tsp superfine sugar
1 tomato, chopped

1 Heat the oil for the beans in a large skillet. Add the onion and sauté for 3–5 minutes. Add the garlic and chili and cook for 1 minute.

2 Mash the beans with a potato masher and stir into the pan with the cilantro.

3 Stir in the stock and cook the beans, stirring, for 5 minutes until soft and pulpy.

4 Place the tortillas on a baking sheet and heat through in a warm oven for 1–2 minutes.

5 Mix the relish ingredients together.

6 Spoon the beans into a serving dish and top with the cheese. Season well. Roll the tortillas and serve with the relish and beans.

COOK'S TIP

Add a little more liquid to the beans when they are cooking if they begin to catch on the bottom of the skillet.

Cabbage & Walnut Stir-Fry

This is a really quick, one-pan dish using white and red cabbage for color and flavor.

Serves 4

INGREDIENTS

12 oz white cabbage
12 oz red cabbage
4 tbsp peanut oil
1 tbsp walnut oil
2 garlic cloves, minced
8 scallion, trimmed

8 oz firm bean curd, cubed
2 tbsp lemon juice
3$^{1}/_{2}$ oz walnut halves
2 tsp Dijon mustard
2 tsp poppy seeds
salt and pepper

1 Using a sharp knife, shred the white and red cabbages thinly and set aside until required.

2 Heat the peanut and walnut oils in a preheated wok. Add the garlic, cabbage, scallion, and bean curd and cook for 5 minutes, stirring.

3 Add the lemon juice, walnuts, and mustard, season with salt and pepper and cook for a further 5 minutes or until the cabbage is tender.

4 Transfer the stir-fry to a warm serving bowl, sprinkle with poppy seeds and serve.

COOK'S TIP

As well as adding protein, vitamins, and useful fats to the diet, nuts and seeds add flavor and texture to vegetarian meals. Keep a good supply of them in your store-cupboard as they can be used in a great variety of dishes – salads, bakes, stir-fries to name but a few.

VARIATION

Sesame seeds could be used instead of the poppy seeds and drizzle 1 teaspoon of sesame oil over the dish just before serving, if you wish.

Tagliarini with Gorgonzola

This simple, creamy pasta sauce is a classic Italian recipe.

Serves 4

INGREDIENTS

2 tbsp butter

8 oz Gorgonzola cheese, roughly
  crumbled

$5/8$ cup heavy cream

2 tbsp dry white wine

1 tsp cornstarch

4 fresh sage sprigs, finely chopped

14 oz dried tagliarini

2 tbsp olive oil

salt and white pepper

1 Melt the butter in a heavy-bottomed saucepan. Stir in 6 oz of the Gorgonzola cheese and melt, over a low heat, for about 2 minutes.

2 Add the cream, wine, and cornstarch and beat with a whisk until fully incorporated.

3 Stir in the sage and season to taste with salt and white pepper. Bring to a boil over a low heat, whisking constantly, until the sauce thickens. Remove from the heat and set aside while you cook the pasta.

4 Bring a large saucepan of lightly salted water to a boil. Add the tagliarini and 1 tbsp of the olive oil. Cook the pasta for 12–14 minutes or until just tender, drain thoroughly, and toss in the remaining olive oil. Transfer the pasta to a serving dish and keep warm.

5 Return the saucepan containing the sauce to a low heat to reheat the sauce, whisking constantly. Spoon the Gorgonzola sauce over the tagliarini, generously sprinkle over the remaining cheese and serve immediately.

COOK'S TIP

Gorgonzola is one of the world's oldest veined cheeses and, arguably, its finest. When buying, always check that it is creamy yellow with delicate green veining. Avoid hard or discolored cheese. It should have a rich, piquant aroma, not a bitter smell. If you find Gorgonzola too strong or rich, you could substitute Danish blue.

Spaghetti with Ricotta Cheese

This light pasta dish has a delicate flavor
ideally suited to a summer lunch.

Serves 4

INGREDIENTS

12 oz dried spaghetti

3 tbsp olive oil

3 tbsp butter

2 tbsp chopped fresh flat leaf parsley

1 cup freshly ground almonds

$^{1}/_{2}$ cup ricotta cheese

pinch of grated nutmeg

pinch of ground cinnamon

$^{5}/_{8}$ cup unsweetened yogurt

4 fl oz hot chicken stock

1 tbsp pine nuts

salt and pepper

fresh flat leaf parsley sprigs,
to garnish

1 Bring a large pan of lightly salted water to a boil. Add the spaghetti and 1 tbsp of the oil and cook until tender, but still firm to the bite.

2 Drain the pasta, return to the pan, and toss with the butter and chopped parsley. Set aside and keep warm.

3 To make the sauce, mix together the ground almonds, ricotta cheese, nutmeg, cinnamon, and unsweetened yogurt over a low heat to form a thick paste. Gradually stir in the remaining oil. When the oil has been fully incorporated, gradually stir in the hot chicken stock, until smooth. Season to taste with black pepper.

4 Transfer the spaghetti to a warm serving dish, pour over the sauce and toss together well (see Cook's Tip, right). Sprinkle over the pine nuts, garnish with the flat leaf parsley, and serve warm.

COOK'S TIP

Use two large forks to toss spaghetti or other long pasta, so that it is thoroughly coated with the sauce. Special spaghetti forks are available from some cookware departments and kitchen stores. Holding one fork in each hand, gently ease the prongs under the pasta on each side and lift them towards the center. Continue this evenly and rhythmically until the pasta is completely coated.

Vegetable Spaghetti with Lemon Dressing

Steaming vegetables helps to preserve their nutritional content and allow them to retain their bright, natural colors, and crunchy texture.

Serves 4

INGREDIENTS

8 oz celeriac
2 medium carrots
2 medium leeks
1 small red bell pepper
1 small yellow bell pepper
2 garlic cloves
1 tsp celery seeds

1 tbsp lemon juice
10 $^1/_2$ oz spaghetti
celery leaves, chopped, to garnish

LEMON DRESSING:
1 tsp finely grated lemon rind
1 tbsp lemon juice

4 tbsp low-fat unsweetened yogurt
salt and pepper
2 tbsp snipped fresh chives

1 Peel the celeriac and carrots, cut into thin matchsticks and place in a bowl. Trim and slice the leeks, rinse under running water to flush out any trapped dirt, then shred finely. Halve, seed, and slice the bell peppers. Peel and thinly slice the garlic. Add all of the vegetables to the bowl with the celeriac and the carrots.

2 Toss the vegetables with the celery seeds and lemon juice.

3 Bring a large saucepan of water to a boil and cook the spaghetti according to the directions on the packet. Drain and keep warm.

4 Meanwhile, bring another large saucepan of water to a boil, put the vegetables in a steamer or strainer and place over the boiling water. Cover and steam for 6–7 minutes or until just tender.

5 When the spaghetti and vegetables are cooked, mix the ingredients for the lemon dressing together.

6 Transfer the spaghetti and vegetables into a warm serving bowl and mix with the dressing. Garnish with chopped celery leaves and serve.

Spaghetti with Anchovy & Pesto Sauce

This is an ideal dish for cooks in a hurry and for those who do not have much time for shopping, as it is prepared in minutes from store-cupboard ingredients.

Serves 4

INGREDIENTS

3 fl oz olive oil
2 garlic cloves, minced
2 oz can anchovy fillets, drained
1 lb dried spaghetti
2 oz pesto sauce (store bought)

2 tbsp finely chopped fresh oregano
1 cup grated Parmesan cheese, plus
  extra for serving (optional)

salt and pepper

2 fresh oregano sprigs, to garnish

1 Reserve 1 tbsp of the oil and heat the remainder in a small saucepan. Add the garlic and fry for 3 minutes.

2 Lower the heat, stir in the anchovies and cook, stirring occasionally, until the anchovies have disintegrated.

3 Bring a large saucepan of lightly salted water to a boil. Add the spaghetti and the remaining olive oil and cook until just tender, but still firm to the bite.

4 Add the pesto sauce and chopped fresh oregano to the anchovy mixture and then season with black pepper to taste.

5 Drain the spaghetti, using a draining spoon, and transfer to a warm serving dish. Pour the pesto sauce over the spaghetti and then sprinkle over the grated Parmesan cheese.

6 Garnish with oregano sprigs and serve with extra cheese, if using.

COOK'S TIP

If you find canned anchovies much too salty, soak them in a saucer of cold milk for 5 minutes, drain and pat dry with kitchen towels before using.

VARIATION

For a vegetarian alternative of this recipe, simply substitute drained sun-dried tomatoes for the anchovy fillets.

Pasta Provençale

A combination of vegetables tossed in a tomato dressing, served on a bed of assorted salad leaves, makes a tasty main meal or an appetizing side dish.

Serves 4

INGREDIENTS

8 oz penne
1 tbsp olive oil
1 oz pitted black olive, drained and chopped
1 oz dry-pack sun-dried tomatoes, soaked, drained and chopped
3¹/₂ oz assorted baby salad leaves
14 oz can artichoke hearts, drained and halved

4 oz baby zucchini, trimmed and sliced
4 oz baby plum tomatoes, halved
salt and pepper
shredded basil leaves, to garnish

DRESSING:
4 tbsp sieved tomatoes
2 tbsp low-fat unsweetened yogurt

1 tbsp unsweetened orange juice
1 small bunch fresh basil, shredded

1 Cook the penne according to the directions on the packet. Do not overcook the pasta – it should still have 'bite'. Drain well and return to the pan. Stir in the olive oil, salt and pepper, olives, and sun-dried tomatoes. Leave to cool.

2 Gently mix the artichokes, zucchini, and plum tomatoes into the cooked pasta. Arrange the salad leaves in a serving bowl.

3 To make the dressing, mix all the ingredients together and toss into the vegetables and pasta.

4 Spoon the mixture on top of the salad leaves and garnish with shredded basil leaves.

VARIATION

For a non-vegetarian version, stir 8 oz canned tuna in brine, drained, and flaked, into the pasta together with the vegetables. Other pasta shapes can be included – look out for farfalle and rotelle.

Mexican-Style Pizzas

Ready-made pizza bases are topped with a chili-flavored tomato sauce and topped with kidney beans, cheese, and jalapeño chilies in this blend of American, Italian, and Mexican cooking.

Serves 4

INGREDIENTS

4 x ready-made individual
   pizza bases
1 tbsp olive oil
7 oz can chopped tomatoes with
   garlic and herbs
2 tbsp tomato paste

7 oz can kidney beans, drained and
   rinsed
4 oz corn nuts, thawed if frozen
1–2 tsp chili sauce
1 large red onion, shredded
3$^{1}/_{2}$ oz reduced-fat Cheddar cheese,

   grated
1 large green chili, sliced into rings
2 tbsp fresh cilantro, chopped
salt and pepper

1 Preheat the oven to 425°F. Arrange the pizza bases on a baking sheet and brush them lightly with the oil.

2 In a bowl, mix together the chopped tomatoes, tomato paste, kidney beans, and corn, and add chili sauce to taste. Season with salt and pepper.

3 Spread the tomato and kidney bean mixture evenly over each pizza base to cover. Top each pizza with shredded onion and sprinkle with some grated cheese and a few slices of green chili to taste. Bake in the oven for about 20 minutes until the vegetables are tender, the cheese has melted and the base is crisp and golden.

4 Remove the pizzas from the baking sheet and transfer to serving plates. Sprinkle with chopped cilantro and serve immediately.

COOK'S TIP

For a low-fat Mexican-style salad to serve with this pizza, arrange sliced tomatoes, fresh cilantro leaves and a few slices of a small, ripe avocado. Sprinkle with fresh lime juice and coarse sea salt. Avocados have quite a high oil content, so eat in moderation.

Pasta Niçoise Salad

Based on the classic French salad niçoise, this recipe contains pasta instead of potatoes.
The very light olive oil dressing has the tang of capers and the fragrance of fresh basil.

Serves 4

INGREDIENTS

8 oz farfalle
6 oz green beans, topped and tailed
12 oz fresh tuna steaks
4 oz baby plum tomatoes, halved
8 anchovy fillets, drained on
   absorbent paper towels
2 tbsp capers in brine, drained
1 oz pitted black olives in brine,

drained
fresh basil leaves, to garnish
salt and pepper

DRESSING:
1 tbsp olive oil
1 garlic clove, minced
1 tbsp lemon juice
$1/2$ tsp finely grated lemon rind
1 tbsp shredded fresh basil leaves

1 Cook the pasta in lightly salted boiling water according to the directions on the packet until just cooked. Drain well, set aside and keep warm.

2 Bring a small saucepan of lightly salted water to a boil and cook the green beans for 5–6 minutes until just tender. Drain well and toss into the pasta. Set aside and keep warm.

3 Preheat the broiler to medium. Rinse and pat the tuna steaks dry on absorbent paper towels. Season on both sides with black pepper. Place the tuna steaks on the broiler rack and cook for 4–5 minutes on each side until cooked through.

4 Drain the tuna on absorbent paper towels and flake into bite-sized pieces. Toss the tuna into the pasta along with the tomatoes, anchovies, capers, and olives. Set aside and keep warm.

5 Meanwhile, prepare the dressing. Mix all the ingredients together and season well. Pour the dressing over the pasta mixture and mix carefully. Transfer to a warmed serving bowl and serve sprinkled with fresh basil leaves.

Root Vegetable Salad

This colorful salad of grated vegetables is perfect for a light starter.
The peppery flavors of the daikon and radishes are refreshingly pungent.
Serve with some toasted bread and assorted salad leaves.

Serves 4

INGREDIENTS

12 oz carrots
8 oz daikon
4 oz radishes
12 oz celeriac
1 tbsp orange juice
2 stalks celery with leaves, washed
    and trimmed

3^1/$_2$ oz assorted salad greens
1 oz walnut pieces

DRESSING:
1 tbsp walnut oil
1 tbsp white wine vinegar
1 tsp whole-grain mustard

^{1}/$_2$ tsp finely grated orange rind
1 tsp celery seeds
salt and pepper

1 Peel and coarsely grate or very finely shred the carrots, daikon, and radishes. Set aside in separate bowls.

2 Peel and coarsely grate or finely shred the celeriac and mix with the orange juice.

3 Remove the celery leaves and reserve. Finely chop the celery stalks.

4 Divide the salad leaves among 4 serving plates and arrange the vegetables in small piles on top. Set aside while you make the dressing.

5 Mix all of the dressing ingredients together and season well. Drizzle a little over each salad. Shred the reserved celery leaves and sprinkle over the salad with the walnut pieces.

COOK'S TIP

Also known as Chinese white radish and mooli, daikon resembles a large white parsnip. It has crisp, slightly pungent flesh, which can be eaten raw or cooked. It is a useful ingredient in stir-fries. Fresh daikon tend to have a stronger flavor than store-bought ones.

Beet & Orange Rice Salad

You must use freshly cooked beet in this unusual combination of colors and flavors. Beet that has been soaked in vinegar will spoil the delicate balance.

Serves 4

INGREDIENTS

1$^1/_3$ cups long-grain and wild rices (see Cook's Tip, below)
4 large oranges
1 lb cooked beet, peeled
2 heads of chicory
salt and pepper

fresh snipped chives, to garnish

DRESSING:
4 tbsp low-fat unsweetened yogurt
1 garlic clove, minced
1 tbsp whole-grain mustard

$^1/_2$ tsp finely grated orange rind
2 tsp clear honey

1 Cook the rices according to the directions on the packet. Drain and set aside to cool.

2 Meanwhile, slice the top and bottom off each orange. Using a sharp knife, remove the skin and pith. Holding the orange over a bowl to catch the juice, carefully slice between each segment. Place the segments in a separate bowl. Cover the juice and leave to chill in the refrigerator until required.

3 Drain the beet if necessary and dice into cubes. Mix with the orange segments, cover, and leave to chill.

4 When the rice has cooled, mix in the reserved orange juice and season with salt and pepper to taste.

5 Line 4 serving bowls or plates with the chicory leaves. Spoon over the rice and top with the beet and orange segments.

6 Mix all the dressing ingredients together and spoon over the salad, or serve separately in a bowl, if preferred. Garnish with fresh snipped chives.

COOK'S TIP

Look out for boxes of ready-mixed long-grain and wild rices. Alternatively, cook 1 cup white rice and $^1/_4$ cup wild rice separately.

Potato, Radish, & Cucumber Salad

*The radishes and the herb and mustard dressing give this colorful salad a
mild mustard flavor which complements the potatoes perfectly.*

Serves 4

INGREDIENTS

1 lb new potatoes, scrubbed and
 halved

1/2 cucumber, sliced thinly

2 tsp salt

1 bunch radishes, sliced thinly

DRESSING:

1 tbsp Dijon mustard

2 tbsp olive oil

1 tbsp white wine vinegar

2 tbsp mixed chopped herbs

1 Cook the potatoes in a
saucepan of boiling water for
10-15 minutes or until tender.
Drain and leave to cool.

2 Meanwhile spread out the
cucumber slices on a plate
and sprinkle with the salt. Leave to
stand for 30 minutes, then rinse
under cold running water and pat
dry with paper towels.

3 Arrange the cucumber and
radish slices on a serving plate
in a decorative pattern and pile the
cooked potatoes in the center of
the slices.

4 In a small bowl, mix the
dressing ingredients together.
Pour the dressing over the salad,
tossing well to coat all of the salad
ingredients. Leave to chill in the
refrigerator before serving.

COOK'S TIP

*The cucumber adds not only color
but a real freshness to the salad. It is
salted and left to stand to remove
the excess water which would make
the salad soggy. Wash the cucumber
well to remove all of the salt, before
adding to the salad.*

VARIATION

*Dijon mustard has a mild clean
taste which is perfect for this salad
as it does not overpower the other
flavors. If unavailable, use another
mild mustard – English mustard is
too strong for this salad.*

Sweet Potato & Nut Salad

Pecan nuts with their slightly bitter flavor are mixed with sweet potatoes in this recipe to make a sweet and sour salad with an interesting texture.

Serves 4

INGREDIENTS

1 lb sweet potatoes, diced
2 celery stalks, sliced
4$\frac{1}{2}$ oz celeriac, grated
2 scallion, sliced
1$\frac{3}{4}$ oz pecan nuts, chopped
2 heads chicory, separated

1 tsp lemon juice
thyme sprigs, to garnish

DRESSING:
4 tbsp vegetable oil
1 tbsp garlic-wine vinegar

1 tsp soft light brown sugar
2 tsp chopped fresh thyme

---

1 Cook the sweet potatoes in a saucepan of boiling water for 5 minutes until tender. Drain thoroughly and leave to cool.

2 When cooled, stir in the celery, celeriac, scallion, and pecan nuts.

3 Line a salad plate with the chicory leaves and sprinkle with lemon juice.

4 Spoon the potato mixture into the center of the leaves.

5 In a small bowl, whisk the dressing ingredients together.

6 Pour the dressing over the salad and serve at once, garnished with thyme sprigs.

COOK'S TIP

Sweet potatoes do not store as well as ordinary potatoes. It is best to store them in a cool, dark place (not the refrigerator) and use within 1 week of purchase.

VARIATION

For variety, replace the garlic wine vinegar in the dressing with a different flavored oil, such as chili or herb.

Potato & Mixed Vegetable Salad with Lemon Mayonnaise

This salad is a medley of crunchy vegetables, mixed with sliced cooked potatoes and ham, then coated in a fresh-tasting lemon mayonnaise. Vary the vegetables according to availability or preference.

Serves 4

INGREDIENTS

1 lb waxy new potatoes, scrubbed
1 carrot, cut into matchsticks
8 oz cauliflower florets
8 oz baby-corn-on-the-cobs, halved
  lengthways
6 oz dwarf beans
6 oz ham, diced

$1^3/4$ oz mushrooms, sliced
salt and pepper

DRESSING:
2 tbsp chopped fresh parsley
$^2/3$ cup mayonnaise
$^2/3$ cup natural yogurt

4 tsp lemon juice
rind of 1 lemon
2 tsp fennel seeds

1 Cook the potatoes in a pan of boiling water for 15 minutes or until tender. Drain and leave to cool. When the potatoes are cold, slice them thinly.

2 Meanwhile, cook the carrot matchsticks, cauliflower florets, baby-corn-on-the-cobs, and dwarf beans in a pan of boiling water for 5 minutes. Drain well and leave to cool.

3 Reserve 1 tsp of the chopped parsley for the garnish. In a bowl, mix the remaining dressing ingredients together.

4 Arrange the vegetables on a salad platter and top with the ham strips and sliced mushrooms.

5 Spoon the dressing over the the salad and garnish with the reserved parsley. Serve at once.

COOK'S TIP

For a really quick salad, use a frozen packet of mixed vegetables, thawed, instead of fresh vegetables.

Potato, Mixed Bean, & Apple Salad

*Use any mixture of beans you have to hand in this recipe;
the wider the variety, the more colorful the salad.*

Serves 4

INGREDIENTS

8 oz new potatoes, scrubbed and
   quartered
8 oz mixed canned beans, such as red
   kidney beans, small navy, and
   borlotti beans, drained and rinsed

1 red eating apple, diced and tossed
   in 1 tbsp lemon juice
1 small yellow bell pepper, diced
1 shallot, sliced
$^1/_2$ head fennel, sliced
oak leaf lettuce leaves

DRESSING:
1 tbsp red wine vinegar
2 tbsp olive oil
$^1/_2$ tbsp American mustard
1 garlic clove, minced
2 tsp chopped fresh thyme

1 Cook the quartered potatoes
in a saucepan of boiling water
for 15 minutes until tender. Drain
and transfer to a mixing bowl.

2 Add the mixed beans to the
potatoes with the diced apple
and yellow bell pepper, and the
sliced shallots and fennel. Mix
well, taking care not to break up
the cooked potatoes.

3 In a bowl, whisk all the
dressing ingredients together,
then pour it over the potato salad.

4 Line a plate or salad bowl
with the oak leaf and spoon
the potato mixture into the center.
Serve immediately.

COOK'S TIP

*Canned beans are used here for
convenience, but dried beans may
be used instead. Soak for 8 hours or
overnight, drain, and place in a
saucepan. Cover with water, bring
to a boil, and boil for 10 minutes,
then simmer until tender.*

VARIATION

*Use Dijon or whole-grain mustard
in place of American mustard for a
different flavor.*

Potato, Arugula, & Apple Salad

This green and white salad is made with creamy, salty-flavored goat's cheese – its distinctive flavor is perfect with salad greens.

Serves 4

INGREDIENTS

2 large potatoes, unpeeled and
  sliced
2 green eating apples, diced
1 tsp lemon juice
1 oz walnut pieces
4^1/$_2$ oz goat's cheese, cubed

5^1/$_2$ oz arugula leaves
salt and pepper

DRESSING:
2 tbsp olive oil
1 tbsp red wine vinegar

1 tsp clear honey
1 tsp fennel seeds

1 Cook the potatoes in a pan of boiling water for 15 minutes until tender. Drain and leave to cool. Transfer the cooled potatoes to a serving bowl.

2 Toss the diced apples in the lemon juice, drain and stir into the cold potatoes.

3 Add the walnut pieces, cheese cubes, and arugula leaves, then toss the salad to mix.

4 In a small bowl, whisk the dressing ingredients together and pour the dressing over the salad. Serve immediately.

COOK'S TIP

Serve this salad immediately to prevent the apple from discoloring. Alternatively, prepare all of the other ingredients in advance and add the apple at the last minute.

VARIATION

Use smoked or blue cheese instead of goat's cheese, if you prefer. In addition, if arugula is unavailable use baby spinach instead.

Minted Fennel Salad

This is a very refreshing salad. The subtle liquorice flavor of fennel combines well with the cucumber and mint.

Serves 4

INGREDIENTS

1 bulb fennel	1 small or ½ a large cucumber	1 tbsp virgin olive oil
2 small oranges	1 tbsp chopped mint	2 eggs, hard cooked

1 Using a sharp knife, trim the outer leaves from the fennel. Slice the fennel bulb thinly into a bowl of water and sprinkle with lemon juice (see Cook's Tip).

2 Grate the rind of the oranges over a bowl. Using a sharp knife, pare away the orange peel, then segment the orange by carefully slicing between each line of pith. Do this over the bowl in order to retain the juice.

3 Cut the cucumber into ½ inch rounds, and cut these into quarters. Add the cucumber and mint to the fennel and orange mixture.

4 Pour the olive oil over the fennel and cucumber salad and toss well.

5 Peel and quarter the eggs and use these to decorate the top of the salad. Serve at once.

COOK'S TIP

Virgin olive oil, which has a fine aroma and flavor, is made by the cold pressing of olives. However, it may have a slightly higher acidity level than extra virgin oil.

COOK'S TIP

Fennel will discolor if it is left for any length of time without a dressing. To prevent any discoloration, place it in a bowl of water and sprinkle with lemon juice.

Yellow Bell Pepper Salad

A colorful combination of yellow bell peppers, red radishes, and celery combine to give a wonderfully crunchy texture and fresh taste.

Serves 4

INGREDIENTS

4 rashers streaky bacon, chopped
2 yellow bell peppers
8 radishes, washed and trimmed

1 stalk celery, finely chopped
3 plum tomatoes, cut into wedges
3 tbsp olive oil

1 tbsp fresh thyme

1 Dry fry the chopped bacon in a skillet for 4–5 minutes or until crispy. Remove the bacon from the skillet, set aside and leave to cool until required.

2 Using a sharp knife, halve and seed the bell peppers. Slice the bell peppers into long strips.

3 Using a sharp knife, halve the radishes and cut them into wedges.

4 Mix together the bell peppers, radishes, celery, and tomatoes and toss the mixture in the olive oil and fresh thyme. Season to taste with a little salt and pepper.

5 Transfer the salad to serving plates and garnish with the reserved crispy bacon.

COOK'S TIP

Tomatoes are actually berries and are related to potatoes. There are many different shapes and sizes of this versatile fruit. The one most used in Italian cooking is the plum tomato which is very flavorsome.

COOK'S TIP

Pre-packaged diced bacon can be purchased from most supermarkets, which helps to save on preparation time.

Old English Spicy Chicken Salad

For this simple, refreshing summer salad you can use leftover roast chicken, or ready-roasted chicken to save time. Add the dressing just before serving, or the spinach will lose its crispness.

Serves 4

INGREDIENTS

9 oz young spinach leaves
3 stalks celery, sliced thinly
1/2 cucumber
2 scallion
3 tbsp chopped fresh parsley
12 oz boneless, roast chicken,
  sliced thinly

DRESSING:
1 inch piece gingerroot, grated finely
3 tbsp olive oil
1 tbsp white wine vinegar
1 tbsp clear honey
1/2 tsp ground cinnamon
salt and pepper

smoked almonds, to garnish
(optional)

1 Thoroughly wash the spinach leaves, then pat dry with paper towels.

2 Using a sharp knife, thinly slice the celery, cucumber, and scallion. Toss in a large bowl with the spinach leaves and parsley.

3 Transfer to serving plates and arrange the chicken on top of the salad.

4 In a screw-topped jar, combine all the dressing ingredients and shake well to mix. Season the dressing with salt and pepper to taste, then pour over the salad. Sprinkle with a few smoked almonds, if using.

VARIATION

Substitute corn salad for the spinach, if you prefer.

VARIATION

Fresh young spinach leaves go particularly well with fruit – try adding a few fresh raspberries or nectarine slices to make an even more refreshing salad.

Indonesian Potato & Chicken Salad

*The spicy peanut dressing served with this salad may be prepared
in advance and left to chill a day before required.*

Serves 4

INGREDIENTS

4 large waxy potatoes, diced
10 oz fresh pineapple, diced
2 carrots, grated
6 oz mung beansprouts
1 bunch scallion, sliced

1 large zucchini, cut into matchsticks
3 celery stalks, cut into matchsticks
6 oz unsalted peanuts
2 cooked chicken breast fillets, about
$4^{1}/_{2}$ oz each, sliced

DRESSING:
6 tbsp crunchy peanut butter
6 tbsp olive oil
2 tbsp light soy sauce
1 red chili, chopped
2 tsp sesame oil
4 tsp lime juice

1 Cook the diced potatoes in a saucepan of boiling water for 10 minutes or until tender. Drain and leave to cool.

2 Transfer the cooled potatoes to a salad bowl.

3 Add the pineapple, carrots, beansprouts, scallion, zucchini, celery, peanuts, and sliced chicken to the potatoes. Toss well to mix all the salad ingredients together.

4 To make the dressing, put the peanut butter in a small bowl and gradually whisk in the olive oil and light soy sauce.

5 Stir in the chopped red chili, sesame oil and lime juice. Mix until well combined.

6 Pour the spicy dressing over the salad and toss lightly to coat all of the ingredients. Serve the salad immediately, garnished with the lime wedges.

COOK'S TIP

Unsweetened canned pineapple may be used in place of the fresh pineapple for convenience. If only sweetened canned pineapple is available, drain it and rinse under cold running water before using.

Potato & Italian Sausage Salad

Sliced Italian sausage blends well with the other Mediterranean flavors of sun-dried tomato and basil in this salad. All of the flavors are relatively strong and therefore do not overpower each other.

Serves 4

INGREDIENTS

1 lb waxy potatoes
1 raddichio or lollo rosso lettuce
1 green bell pepper, sliced
6 oz Italian sausage, sliced
1 red onion, halved and sliced

4$^1/_2$ oz sun-dried tomatoes, sliced
2 tbsp shredded fresh basil

DRESSING:
1 tbsp balsamic vinegar
1 tsp tomato paste
2 tbsp olive oil
salt and pepper

1 Cook the potatoes in a saucepan of boiling water for 20 minutes or until cooked through. Drain and leave to cool.

2 Line a large serving platter with the radicchio or lollo rosso lettuce leaves.

3 Slice the cooled potatoes and arrange them in layers on the lettuce-lined serving platter together with the sliced green bell pepper, sliced Italian sausage, red onion, sun-dried tomatoes, and shredded fresh basil.

4 In a small bowl, whisk the balsamic vinegar, tomato paste, and olive oil together and season to taste with salt and pepper. Pour the dressing over the potato salad and serve immediately.

COOK'S TIP

You can use either packets of sun-dried tomatoes or jars of sun-dried tomatoes in oil. If using tomatoes packed in oil, simply rinse the oil from the tomatoes and pat them dry on paper towels before using.

VARIATION

Any sliced Italian sausage or salami can be used in this salad. Italy is home of the salami and there are numerous varieties to choose from – those from the south tend to be more highly spiced than those from the north of the country.

Lentil & Tuna Salad

In this recipe, lentils, combined with spices, lemon juice, and tuna, make a wonderfully tasty and filling salad.

Serves 4

INGREDIENTS

3 tbsp virgin olive oil
1 tbsp lemon juice
1 tsp whole-grain mustard
1 garlic clove, minced

$^1/_2$ tsp cumin powder
$^1/_2$ tsp ground coriander
1 small red onion
2 ripe tomatoes
1 x 14 oz can lentils, drained

1 x 6$^1/_2$ can tuna, drained
2 tbsp fresh cilantro, chopped
pepper

1 Using a sharp knife, seed the tomatoes and chop them into fine dice.

2 Using a sharp knife, finely chop the red onion.

3 To make the dressing, whisk together the virgin olive oil, lemon juice, mustard, garlic, cumin powder, and ground coriander in a small bowl. Set aside until required.

4 Mix together the chopped onion, diced tomatoes, and drained lentils in a large bowl.

5 Flake the tuna and stir it into the onion, tomato, and lentil mixture.

6 Stir in the chopped fresh cilantro.

7 Pour the dressing over the lentil and tuna salad and season with freshly ground black pepper. Serve at once.

VARIATION

Nuts would add extra flavor and texture to this salad.

COOK'S TIP

Lentils are a good source of protein and contain important vitamins and minerals. Buy them dried for soaking and cooking yourself, or buy canned varieties for speed and convenience.

Chinese Shrimp Salad

Noodles and beansprouts form the basis of this refreshing salad which combines the flavors of fruit and shrimp for a quick and delicious dish.

Serves 4

INGREDIENTS

9 oz fine egg noodles
3 tbsp sunflower oil
1 tbsp sesame oil
1 tbsp sesame seeds

1$\frac{1}{2}$ cups mung beansprouts
1 ripe mango, sliced
6 scallion, sliced
2$\frac{3}{4}$ oz radish, sliced

12 oz peeled cooked shrimp
2 tbsp light soy sauce
1 tbsp sherry

1 Place the egg noodles in a large bowl and pour over enough boiling water to cover. Leave to stand for 10 minutes.

2 Drain the noodles thoroughly and pat away any moisture with absorbent paper towels.

3 Heat the sunflower oil in a large wok. Add the noodles and stir-fry for 5 minutes, tossing frequently.

4 Remove the wok from the heat and add the sesame oil, sesame seeds and beansprouts, tossing to mix well.

5 In a separate bowl, mix together the sliced mango, scallion, radish, shrimp, light soy sauce, and sherry.

6 Toss the shrimp mixture with the noodles or alternatively, arrange the noodles around the edge of a serving plate and pile the shrimp mixture into the center. Serve immediately.

VARIATION

If fresh mango is unavailable, use canned mango slices, rinsed and drained, instead.

Meat & Poultry

There is a wide variety of meat recipes in this chapter, and in many cases the meat is lamb. I prefer to use leg of lamb, as it contains much less fat than shoulder, but if you like shoulder, I suggest you combine it with an equal proportion of leg, which works very well. In some of the recipes beef (braising steak, for example) may be substituted for lamb, but if you do this you will need to allow a little extra cooking time.

In India, chicken is expensive and is therefore considered a special-occasion meat. A chicken dish is invariably served at every function. Indians always cook chicken skinned and cut into small pieces. If the chicken weighs about 3 lb 5 oz it should be cut into about 8 pieces, unless you are making Tandoori Chicken, when chicken quarters look a lot better and are more appropriate.

Honey-Glazed Pork Chops

The addition of freshly grated ginger gives a delicious tang to the honey-flavored glaze.

Serves 6

INGREDIENTS

4 lean pork loin chops
4 tbsp clear honey
1 tbsp dry sherry

4 tbsp orange juice
2 tbsp olive oil
1 inch piece gingerroot, grated
salt and pepper

1 Season the pork chops with salt and pepper to taste. Set aside while you make the glaze.

2 To make the glaze, place the honey, sherry, orange juice, oil, and ginger in a small pan and heat gently, stirring continuously, until all of the ingredients are well blended.

3 grill the chops on an oiled rack over hot coals for about 5 minutes on each side.

4 Brush the chops with the glaze and grill for a further 2–4 minutes on each side, basting frequently with the glaze.

5 Transfer the chops to warm serving plates and serve hot.

VARIATION

This recipe works equally well with lamb chops and with chicken portions, such as thighs or drumsticks. grill the meat in exactly the same way as in this recipe, basting frequently with the honey glaze – the result will be just as delicious!.

COOK'S TIP

To give the recipe a little more punch, stir $\frac{1}{2}$ teaspoon of chili sauce or 1 tablespoon of wholegrain mustard to the basting glaze.

Caribbean Pork

...l dish combines the sweetness of fruit juices with the sharpness of rum. It is excellent served with typically Caribbean coconut rice.

Serves 6

INGREDIENTS

4 pork loin chops
4 tbsp dark muscovado sugar
4 tbsp orange or pineapple juice
2 tbsp Jamaican rum
1 tbsp crushed coconut
1 tsp ground cinnamon

mixed salad leaves, to serve

COCONUT RICE:
1 cup Basmati rice
2 cups water
1 cup coconut milk

4 tbsp raisins
4 tbsp roasted peanuts
salt and pepper
2 tbsp crushed coconut, toasted

1 Trim any excess fat from the pork and place the chops in a shallow, non-metallic dish.

2 Combine the sugar, fruit juice, rum, coconut, and cinnamon in a bowl, stirring until the sugar dissolves. Pour the mixture over the pork and leave to marinate in the refrigerator for at least two hours.

3 Remove the pork from the marinade, reserving the liquid for basting. Grill over hot coals for 15-20 minutes, basting with the marinade.

4 Meanwhile, make the coconut rice. Rinse the rice under cold water, place it in a pan with the water and coconut milk, and bring it gently to a boil. Stir, cover, and reduce the heat. Simmer gently for 12 minutes or until the rice is tender and the liquid has been absorbed. Fluff up with a fork.

5 Stir the raisins and nuts into the rice, season with salt and pepper to taste, and sprinkle with the coconut. Transfer the pork and rice to warm serving plates and serve with the mixed salad leaves.

Twice-Cooked Pork with Bell Peppers

This is a really simple yet colorful dish, the trio of bell peppers off-setting the pork and sauce wonderfully.

Serves 4

INGREDIENTS

¹/₂ oz dried shiitake mushrooms	1 red bell pepper, seeded and diced	4 tbsp oyster sauce
1 lb pork leg steaks	1 green bell pepper, seeded and diced	
2 tbsp vegetable oil	1 yellow bell pepper, seeded and diced	
1 onion, sliced		

1 Place the mushrooms in a large bowl. Pour over enough boiling water to cover and leave to stand for 20 minutes.

2 Using a sharp knife, trim any excess fat from the pork steaks. Cut the pork into thin strips.

3 Bring a large saucepan of water to a boil. Add the pork to a boiling water and cook for 5 minutes.

4 Remove the pork from the pan with a draining spoon and leave to drain thoroughly.

5 Heat the oil in a large preheated wok. Add the pork to the wok and stir-fry for about 5 minutes.

6 Remove the mushrooms from the water and leave to drain thoroughly. Roughly chop the mushrooms.

7 Add the mushrooms, onion and the bell peppers to the wok and stir-fry for 5 minutes.

8 Stir in the oyster sauce and cook for 2-3 minutes. Transfer to serving bowls and serve immediately.

VARIATION

Use open-cap mushrooms, sliced, instead of shiitake mushrooms, if you prefer.

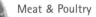

Pork Tenderloin Stir-Fry with Crunchy Satay Sauce

Satay sauce is easy to make and is one of the best known and loved sauces in Oriental cooking. It is perfect with beef, chicken, or pork as in this recipe.

Serves 4

INGREDIENTS

5¹/₂ oz carrots

2 tbsp sunflower oil

12 oz pork neck tenderloin, thinly sliced

1 onion, sliced

2 cloves garlic, minced

1 yellow bell pepper, seeded and sliced

2¹/₃ cups snow peas

1¹/₂ cups fine asparagus

chopped salted peanuts, to serve

SATAY SAUCE:

6 tbsp crunchy peanut butter

6 tbsp coconut milk

1 tsp chili flakes

1 clove garlic, minced

1 tsp tomato paste

1 Using a sharp knife, slice the carrots into thin sticks.

2 Heat the oil in a large wok. Add the pork, onion and garlic and stir-fry for 5 minutes or until the lamb is cooked through.

3 Add the carrots, bell pepper, snow peas, and asparagus to the wok and stir-fry for 5 minutes.

4 To make the satay sauce, place the peanut butter, coconut milk, chili flakes, garlic, and tomato paste in a small pan and heat gently, stirring, until well combined.

5 Transfer the stir-fry to warm serving plates. Spoon the satay sauce over the stir-fry and scatter with chopped peanuts. Serve immediately.

COOK'S TIP

Cook the sauce just before serving as it tends to thicken very quickly and will not be spoonable if you cook it too far in advance.

Pork Fry with Vegetables

This is a very simple dish which lends itself to almost any combination of vegetables that you have to hand.

Serves 4

INGREDIENTS

12 oz lean pork tenderloin
2 tbsp vegetable oil
2 garlic cloves, minced
$1/2$-inch piece gingerroot,
   cut into slivers
1 carrot, cut into thin strips

1 red bell pepper, seeded and diced
1 fennel bulb, sliced
1 oz water chestnuts, halved
$2^3/4$ oz mung beansprouts
2 tbsp Chinese rice wine
$1^1/4$ cups pork or chicken stock

pinch of dark brown sugar
1 tsp cornstarch
2 tsp water

1 Cut the pork into thin slices. Heat the oil in a preheated wok. Add the garlic, ginger, and pork and stir-fry for 1–2 minutes, until the meat is sealed.

2 Add the carrot, bell pepper, fennel, and water chestnuts to the wok and stir-fry for about 2-3 minutes.

3 Add the beansprouts and stir-fry for 1 minute. Remove the pork and vegetables from the wok and keep warm.

4 Add the Chinese rice wine, pork or chicken stock, and sugar to the wok. Blend the cornstarch to a smooth paste with the water and stir it into the sauce. Bring to a boil, stirring constantly until thickened and clear.

5 Return the meat and vegetables to the wok and cook for 1–2 minutes, until heated through and coated with the sauce. Transfer to a warm serving dish and serve immediately.

COOK'S TIP

Use dry sherry instead of the Chinese rice wine if you have difficulty obtaining it.

Orecchioni with Pork in Cream Sauce, Garnished with Quail Eggs

This unusual and attractive dish is surprisingly quick and easy to make.

Serves 4

INGREDIENTS

1 lb pork tenderloin, thinly sliced

4 tbsp olive oil

8 oz button mushrooms, sliced

⁷/₈ cup Italian red wine sauce

1 tbsp lemon juice

pinch of saffron

3 cups dried orecchioni

4 tbsp heavy cream

12 quail eggs (see Cook's Tip, below)

salt

1 Pound the slices of pork between 2 sheets of plastic wrap until they are wafer thin, then cut into strips.

2 Heat the olive oil in a large skillet, add the pork and stir-fry for 5 minutes. Add the mushrooms to the pan and stir-fry for a further 2 minutes.

3 Pour over the Italian red wine sauce, lower the heat, and simmer gently for 20 minutes.

4 Meanwhile, bring a large saucepan of lightly salted water to a boil. Add the lemon juice, saffron, and orecchioni and cook for 12 minutes, until tender but still firm to the bite. Drain the pasta and keep warm.

5 Stir the cream into the pan with the pork and heat gently for a few minutes.

6 Boil the quail eggs for 3 minutes, cool them in cold water and remove the shells.

7 Transfer the pasta to a large, warm serving plate, top with the pork and the sauce and garnish with the eggs. Serve immediately.

COOK'S TIP

In this recipe, the quail eggs are soft-cooked. As they are extremely difficult to shell when warm, it is important that they are thoroughly cooled first. Otherwise, they will break up unattractively.

Neapolitan Pork Steaks

An Italian version of grilled pork steaks, this dish is easy to make and delicious to eat.

Serves 4

INGREDIENTS

2 tbsp olive oil
1 garlic clove, chopped
1 large onion, sliced
1 x 14 oz can tomatoes

2 tsp yeast extract
4 pork loin steaks,
  each about 4^1/$_2$ oz
2 ^{3}/$_4$ oz black olives, pitted

2 tbsp fresh basil, shredded
freshly grated Parmesan cheese, to
  serve

1 Heat the oil in a large skillet. Add the onions and garlic and cook, stirring, for 3–4 minutes or until they just begin to soften.

2 Add the tomatoes and yeast extract to the skillet and leave to simmer for about 5 minutes or until the sauce starts to thicken.

3 Cook the pork steaks, under a preheated broiler, for 5 minutes on both sides, until the the meat is golden and cooked through. Set the pork steaks aside and keep warm.

4 Add the olives and fresh shredded basil to the sauce in the skillet and stir quickly to combine.

5 Transfer the steaks to warm serving plates. Top the steaks with the sauce, sprinkle with freshly grated Parmesan cheese and serve immediately.

COOK'S TIP

Parmesan is a mature and exceptionally hard cheese produced in Italy. You only need to add a little as it has a very strong flavor.

COOK'S TIP

There are many types of canned tomato available – for example plum tomatoes, or tomatoes chopped in water, or chopped sieved passata. The chopped variety are often canned with added flavors such as garlic, basil, onion, chili, and mixed herbs, and are a good storecupboard standby.

Ham Steaks with Spicy Apple Rings

This dish is quick to prepare because there is no marinating involved. Ham has a good, strong flavor and cooks well on the grill.

Serves 4

INGREDIENTS

4 ham steaks, each about 6 oz
1–2 tsp whole-grain mustard
1 tbsp honey
2 tbsp lemon juice
1 tbsp sunflower oil

APPLE RINGS:
2 green eating apples
2 tsp demerara sugar
1/4 tsp ground nutmeg
1/4 tsp ground cinnamon

1/4 tsp ground allspice
1–2 tbsp melted butter

1 Using a pair of scissors, make a few cuts around the edges of the ham steaks to prevent them from curling up as they cook. Spread a little whole-grain mustard over the steaks.

2 Mix together the honey, lemon juice, and oil in a bowl.

3 To prepare the apple rings, core the apples and cut them into thick slices. Mix the sugar with the spices and press the apple slices in the mixture until well coated on both sides.

4 grill the steaks over hot coals for 3–4 minutes on each side, basting with the honey and lemon mixture.

5 Brush the apple slices with a little melted butter and grill alongside the pork for 3–4 minutes, turning once and brushing with melted butter as they cook.

6 Serve the ham steaks with the apple slices as a garnish.

COOK'S TIP

Ham can be a little salty. If you have time, soak the steaks in cold water for 30–60 minutes before cooking – this process will remove the excess salt.

VARIATION

Pineapple rings can also be cooked in the same way as the apple rings for a delicious alternative garnish to this dish.

Lamb Cutlets with Rosemary

A classic combination of flavors, this dish would make a perfect Sunday lunch.
Serve with tomato and onion salad and jacket potatoes.

Serves 4

INGREDIENTS

8 lamb cutlets

5 tbsp olive oil

2 tbsp lemon juice

1 clove garlic, minced

$^1/_2$ tsp lemon pepper

salt

8 sprigs rosemary

jacket potatoes, to serve

SALAD:

4 tomatoes, sliced

4 scallions, sliced diagonally

DRESSING:

2 tbsp olive oil

1 tbsp lemon juice

1 clove garlic, chopped

$^1/_4$ tsp fresh rosemary, chopped finely

1 Trim the lamb chops by cutting away the flesh with a sharp knife to expose the tips of the bones.

2 Place the oil, lemon juice, garlic, lemon pepper, and salt in a shallow, non-metallic dish and whisk with a fork to combine.

3 Lay the sprigs of rosemary in the dish and place the lamb on top. Leave to marinate for at least 1 hour, turning the lamb cutlets once.

4 Remove the chops from the marinade and wrap a little kitchen foil around the bones to stop them from burning.

5 Place the sprigs of rosemary on the rack and place the lamb on top. grill for 10–15 minutes, turning once.

6 Meanwhile make the salad and dressing. Arrange the tomatoes on a serving dish and scatter the scallions on top. Place all the ingredients for the dressing

in a screw-top jar, shake well and pour over the salad. Serve with the grilled lamb cutlets and jacket potatoes.

COOK'S TIP

Choose medium to small baking potatoes if you want to cook jacket potatoes on the grill. Scrub them well, prick with a fork and wrap in buttered kitchen foil. Bury them in the hot coals and grill for 50–60 minutes.

Scallion & Lamb Stir-Fry with Oyster Sauce

*This really is a speedy dish, lamb leg steaks being perfect
for the short cooking time.*

Serves 4

INGREDIENTS

1 lb lamb leg steaks
1 tsp ground Szechuan peppercorns
1 tbsp peanut oil

2 cloves garlic, minced
8 scallions, sliced
2 tbsp dark soy sauce

6 tbsp oyster sauce
6 oz Chinese cabbage
shrimp crackers, to serve

1 Using a sharp knife, remove any excess fat from the lamb. Slice the lamb thinly.

2 Sprinkle the ground Szechuan peppercorns over the meat and toss together until well combined.

3 Heat the oil in a preheated wok. Add the lamb and stir-fry for 5 minutes.

4 Mix the garlic, scallions, and soy, add to the wok and stir-fry for 2 minutes.

5 Add the oyster sauce and Chinese leaves and stir-fry for a further 2 minutes, or until the leaves have wilted and the juices are bubbling.

6 Transfer the stir-fry to warm serving bowls and serve hot.

COOK'S TIP

Oyster sauce is made from oysters which are cooked in brine and soy sauce. Sold in bottles, it will keep in the refrigerator for months.

COOK'S TIP

shrimp crackers consist of compressed slivers of shrimp and flour paste. They expand when deep-fried.

Lean Lamb Cooked in Spinach

I like to serve this nutritious combination of lamb and spinach with plain boiled rice to bring out the flavor.

Serves 2-4

INGREDIENTS

1¼ cups oil
2 medium onions, sliced
¼ bunch fresh cilantro
3 green chilies, chopped
1½ tsp fresh gingerroot, finely
    chopped
1½ tsp fresh garlic, minced
1 tsp chili powder

½ tsp turmeric
1 lb lean lamb, with or
    without the bone
1 tsp salt
2 lb fresh spinach, trimmed, washed,
    and chopped or 15 oz can spinach
3¼ cups water
TO GARNISH:

fresh gingerroot, peeled and
    shredded
fresh cilantro leaves

1 Heat the oil in a saucepan and fry the onions until they turn a pale color.

2 Add the fresh cilantro and 2 of the chopped green chilies to the pan and stir-fry for 3-5 minutes.

3 Reduce the heat and add the ginger, garlic, chili powder, and turmeric to the mixture in the pan, stirring to mix.

4 Add the lamb to the pan and stir-fry for a further 5 minutes. Add the salt and the fresh or canned spinach and cook, stirring occasionally with a wooden spoon, for a further 3-5 minutes.

5 Add the water, stirring, and cook over a low heat, covered, for about 45 minutes. Remove the lid and check the meat. If it is not tender, turn the meat over,

increase the heat and cook, uncovered, until the surplus water has been absorbed. Stir-fry the mixture for a further 5-7 minutes.

6 Transfer the lamb and spinach mixture to a serving dish and garnish with shredded ginger, fresh cilantro leaves and the remaining chopped green chili. Serve hot.

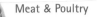

Grilled Ground Lamb

This is rather an unusual way of cooking ground meat. In India this is cooked on a naked flame, but I use my broiler instead and find it works just as well.

Serves 4

INGREDIENTS

5 tbsp oil
2 onions, sliced
1 lb ground lamb
2 tbsp yogurt
1 tsp chili powder
1 tsp fresh gingerroot, finely chopped

1 tsp fresh garlic, minced
1 tsp salt
$1\frac{1}{2}$ tsp garam masala
$\frac{1}{2}$ tsp ground allspice
2 fresh green chilies
fresh cilantro leaves

TO GARNISH:
1 onion, cut into rings
fresh cilantro leaves, chopped
1 lemon, cut into wedges

1 Heat the oil in a saucepan. Add the onions and fry until golden brown.

2 Place the ground lamb in a large bowl. Add the yogurt, chili powder, ginger, garlic, salt, garam masala, ground allspice, and mix to combine.

3 Add the lamb mixture to the fried onions and stir-fry for 10-15 minutes. Remove from the heat and set aside.

4 Meanwhile, place the green chilies and half of the cilantro leaves in a processor and grind. Alternatively, finely chop the green chilies and cilantro with a sharp knife. Set aside until required.

5 Put the ground lamb mixture in a food processor and grind. Alternatively, place in a large bowl and mash with a fork. Mix the lamb mixture with the chilies and cilantro and blend well.

6 Transfer the mixture to a shallow heatproof dish. Cook under a preheated medium-hot broiler for 10-15 minutes, moving the mixture about with a fork. Watch it carefully to prevent it from burning.

7 Serve garnished with onion rings, cilantro, and lemon wedges.

Sesame Lamb Stir-Fry

This is a very simple, but delicious dish, in which lean pieces of lamb are cooked in sugar and soy sauce and sprinkled with sesame seeds, then served on a bed of leeks and carrot.

Serves 4

INGREDIENTS

1 lb boneless lean lamb

2 tbsp peanut oil

2 leeks, sliced

1 carrot, cut into matchsticks

2 garlic cloves, minced

$^1/_3$ cup lamb or vegetable stock

2 tsp light brown sugar

1 tbsp dark soy sauce

4$^1/_2$ tsp sesame seeds

1 Cut the lamb into thin strips. Heat the peanut oil in a preheated wok. Add the lamb and stir-fry for 2–3 minutes. Remove the lamb from the wok with a draining spoon and set aside.

2 Add the leek, carrot, and garlic to the wok and stir-fry in the remaining oil for 1–2 minutes. Remove from the wok with a draining spoon and set aside. Drain any remaining oil from the wok.

3 Place the lamb or vegetable stock, sugar, and soy sauce in the wok and add the lamb. Cook, stirring constantly to coat the lamb, for 2–3 minutes. Sprinkle the sesame seeds over the top, turning the lamb to coat.

4 Spoon the leek mixture on to a warm serving dish and top

VARIATION

This recipe would be equally delicious made with strips of skinless chicken or turkey breast or with shrimp. The cooking times remain the same.

COOK'S TIP

Be careful not to burn the sugar in the wok when heating and coating the meat, otherwise the flavor of the dish will be spoiled.

Lamb with Mushroom Sauce

*Use a lean cut of lamb, such as tenderloin, for this recipe
for both flavor and tenderness.*

Serves 4

INGREDIENTS

12 oz lean boneless lamb, such as
   tenderloin
2 tbsp vegetable oil
3 garlic cloves, minced
1 leek, sliced
1 tsp cornstarch

4 tbsp light soy sauce
3 tbsp Chinese rice wine or
   dry sherry
3 tbsp water
$^1/_2$ tsp chili sauce
6 oz large mushrooms, sliced

$^1/_2$ tsp sesame oil
fresh red chilies, to garnish

1 Using a sharp knife, cut the lamb into thin strips.

2 Heat the oil in a preheated wok. Add the lamb strips, garlic, and leek and stir-fry for about 2-3 minutes.

3 Mix together the cornstarch, soy sauce, Chinese rice wine or dry sherry, water, and chili sauce in a bowl and set aside.

4 Add the mushrooms to the wok and stir-fry for 1 minute.

5 Stir in the sauce and cook for 2–3 minutes, or until the lamb is cooked through and tender. Sprinkle the sesame oil over the top and transfer to a warm serving dish. Garnish with red chilies and serve immediately.

COOK'S TIP

Use rehydrated dried Chinese mushrooms obtainable from specialist stores or Chinese supermarkets for a really authentic flavor.

VARIATION

The lamb can be replaced with lean steak or pork tenderloin in this classic recipe from Beijing. You could also use 2–3 scallions, 1 shallot, or 1 small onion instead of the leek, if you prefer.

Stir-Fried Lamb with Orange

Oranges and lamb are a great combination because the citrus flavor off-sets the fattier, fuller flavor of the lamb.

Serves 4

INGREDIENTS

1 lb ground lamb
2 cloves garlic, minced
1 tsp cumin seeds
1 tsp ground coriander

1 red onion, sliced
finely grated zest and juice of
  1 orange
2 tbsp soy sauce

1 orange, peeled and segmented
salt and pepper
snipped fresh chives, to garnish

1 Add the ground lamb to a preheated wok. Dry fry the ground lamb for 5 minutes, or until the meat is evenly browned. Drain away any excess fat from the wok.

2 Add the garlic, cumin seeds, coriander, and red onion to the wok and stir-fry for a further 5 minutes.

3 Stir in the finely grated orange zest and juice and the soy sauce, cover, reduce the heat, and leave to simmer, stirring occasionally, for 15 minutes.

4 Remove the lid, raise the heat, add the orange segments, and salt and pepper to taste and heat through for a further 2–3 minutes.

5 Transfer to warm serving plates and garnish with snipped fresh chives. Serve immediately.

COOK'S TIP

If you wish to serve wine with your meal, try light, dry white wines and lighter Burgundy-style red wines as they blend well with oriental food.

VARIATION

Use lime or lemon juice and zest instead of the orange, if you prefer.

Sweet Lamb Tenderloin

Lamb tenderloin, enhanced by a sweet and spicy glaze, is cooked in a kitchen foil packet for deliciously moist results.

Serves 4

INGREDIENTS

2 tenderloins, each 8 oz
1 tbsp olive oil
$^1/_2$ onion, chopped finely
1 clove garlic, minced
1 inch piece gingerroot, grated

5 tbsp apple juice
3 tbsp smooth apple sauce
1 tbsp light muscovado sugar
1 tbsp tomato catsup
$^1/_2$ tsp mild mustard

salt and pepper
green salad greens, croutons, and
   fresh crusty bread, to serve

1 Place the lamb tenderloin on a large piece of double thickness kitchen foil. Season with salt and pepper to taste.

2 Heat the oil in a small skillet and fry the onion and garlic for 2–3 minutes until soft but not browned. Stir in the grated ginger and cook for 1 minute, stirring occasionally.

3 Stir in the apple juice, apple sauce, sugar, catsup, and mustard and bring to a boil. Boil rapidly for about 10 minutes until reduced by half. Stir the mixture occasionally so that it does not burn and stick to the bottom.

4 Brush half of the sauce over the lamb, then wrap up the lamb in the kitchen foil to completely enclose it. grill over hot coals for about 25 minutes, turning the packet over from time to time.

5 Open out the kitchen foil and brush the lamb with some of the sauce. Continue to grill for a further 15–20 minutes or until cooked through.

6 Place the lamb on a chopping board, remove the foil, and cut into thick slices. Transfer to serving plates and spoon over the remaining sauce. Serve with green salad greens, croutons, and fresh crusty bread.

COOK'S TIP

If you prefer, you can cook the lamb for the first part of the cooking time in a preheated oven at 350°F. Place the kitchen foil packet in a baking dish to avoid any leakages.

Beef with Green Peas & Black Bean Sauce

This recipe is the perfect example of quick stir-frying ingredients for a delicious, crisp, colorful dish.

Serves 4

INGREDIENTS

1 lb rump steak
2 tbsp sunflower oil
1 onion

2 cloves garlic, minced
1 cup fresh or frozen English peas
5 ³/4 oz jar black bean sauce

5 ¹/2 oz Chinese cabbage, shredded

1 Using a sharp knife, trim away any fat from the beef. Cut the beef into thin slices.

2 Heat the sunflower oil in a large preheated wok.

3 Add the beef to the wok and stir-fry for 2 minutes.

4 Using a sharp knife, peel and slice the onion.

5 Add the onion, garlic, and peas to the wok and stir-fry for a further 5 minutes.

6 Add the black bean sauce and Chinese cabbage to the mixture in the wok and heat through for a further 2 minutes.

7 Transfer to warm serving bowls and serve immediately.

COOK'S TIP

Chinese cabbage are now widely available. They look like a pale, elongated head of lettuce with light green, tightly packed crinkly leaves.

COOK'S TIP

Buy a chunky black bean sauce if you can for the best texture and flavor.

Stir-Fried Beef & Vegetables with Sherry & Soy Sauce

Beef tenderloin is perfect for stir-frying as it is so tender and lends itself to quick cooking.

Serves 4

INGREDIENTS

2 tbsp sunflower oil
12 oz beef tenderloin, sliced
1 red onion, sliced
6 oz zucchini, sliced diagonally
6 oz carrots, thinly sliced
1 red bell pepper, seeded and sliced
1 small head Chinese cabbage,
  shredded

1 1/2 cups mung beansprouts
8 oz can bamboo shoots, drained
1/2 cup cashew nuts, toasted

SAUCE:
3 tbsp medium sherry
3 tbsp light soy sauce
1 tsp ground ginger

1 clove garlic, minced
1 tsp cornstarch
1 tbsp tomato paste

1 Heat the sunflower oil in a large preheated wok.

2 Add the beef and onion to the wok and stir-fry for 4–5 minutes or until the onion begins to soften and the meat is just browning.

3 Using a sharp knife, trim the zucchini and slice diagonally.

4 Add the carrots, bell pepper, and zucchini and stir-fry for 5 minutes.

5 Toss in the Chinese cabbage, beansprouts and bamboo shoots and heat through for 2–3 minutes, or until the leaves are just beginning to wilt.

6 Scatter the cashews nuts over the stir-fry.

7 To make the sauce, mix together the sherry, soy sauce, ground ginger, garlic, cornstarch, and tomato paste. Pour the sauce over the stir-fry and toss until well combined. Allow the sauce to bubble for 2–3 minutes or until the juices start to thicken.

8 Transfer to warm serving dishes and serve at once.

Beef & Beans

The green of the beans complements the dark color
of the beef, served in a rich sauce.

Serves 4

INGREDIENTS

1 lb rump or steak tenderloin, cut
   into 1-inch pieces

MARINADE:
2 tsp cornstarch
2 tbsp dark soy sauce
2 tsp peanut oil

SAUCE:
2 tbsp vegetable oil
3 garlic cloves, minced
1 small onion, cut into 8
8 oz thin dwarf beans, halved
1/4 cup unsalted cashews
1 oz canned bamboo shoots, drained
   and rinsed

2 tsp dark soy sauce
2 tsp Chinese rice wine or dry sherry
1/2 cup beef stock
2 tsp cornstarch
4 tsp water
salt and pepper

1 To make the marinade, mix together the cornstarch, soy sauce, and peanut oil.

2 Place the steak in a shallow glass bowl. Pour the marinade over the steak, turn to coat thoroughly, cover, and leave to marinate in the refrigerator for at least 30 minutes.

3 To make the sauce, heat the oil in a preheated wok. Add the garlic, onion, beans, cashews, and bamboo shoots and stir-fry for 2–3 minutes.

4 Remove the steak from the marinade, drain, add to the wok, and stir-fry for 3–4 minutes.

5 Mix the soy sauce, Chinese rice wine or sherry, and beef stock together. Blend the cornstarch with the water and add to the soy sauce mixture, mixing to combine.

6 Stir the mixture into the wok and bring the sauce to a boil, stirring until thickened and clear. Reduce the heat and leave to simmer for 2–3 minutes. Season to taste and serve immediately.

VARIATION

This recipe would also be delicious with the addition of sugar snap peas instead of the beans, if you prefer.

Beef & Broccoli Stir-Fry

This is a great combination of ingredients in terms of color and flavor,
and it is so simple and quick to prepare.

Serves 4

INGREDIENTS

8 oz lean steak, trimmed

2 garlic cloves, minced

dash of chili oil

^{1}/$_2$-inch piece fresh gingerroot,
   grated

^{1}/$_2$ tsp Chinese five spice powder

2 tbsp dark soy sauce

2 tbsp vegetable oil

5 oz broccoli florets

1 tbsp light soy sauce

^{2}/$_3$ cup beef stock

2 tsp cornstarch

4 tsp water

carrot strips, to garnish

1 Cut the steak into thin strips and place in a shallow glass dish. Mix together the garlic, chili oil, grated ginger, Chinese five spice powder, and soy sauce in a small bowl and pour over the beef, tossing to coat the strips evenly. Leave to marinate in the refrigerator.

2 Heat 1 tablespoon of the vegetable oil in a preheated wok. Add the broccoli and stir-fry over a medium heat for 4–5 minutes. Remove from the wok and set aside.

3 Heat the remaining oil in the wok. Add the steak together with the marinade, and stir-fry for 2-3 minutes, until the steak is browned and sealed.

4 Return the broccoli to the wok and stir in the soy sauce and stock.

5 Blend the cornstarch with the water to form a smooth paste and stir it into the wok. Bring to a boil, stirring, until thickened, and clear. Cook for 1 minute.

COOK'S TIP

Leave the steak to marinate for several hours for a fuller flavor. Cover and leave to marinate in the refrigerator if preparing in advance.

6 Transfer the beef and broccoli stir-fry to a warm serving dish, arrange the carrot strips in a lattice on top and serve immediately.

Spicy Beef

In this recipe beef is marinated in a five-spice and chili marinade for a spicy flavor.

Serves 4

INGREDIENTS

8 oz steak tenderloin
2 garlic cloves, minced
1 tsp powdered star anise
1 tbsp dark soy sauce
scallion tassels, to garnish

SAUCE:
2 tbsp vegetable oil
1 bunch scallions, halved lengthways
1 tbsp dark soy sauce

1 tbsp dry sherry

$^1/_4$ tsp chili sauce
$^2/_3$ cup water
2 tsp cornstarch
4 tsp water

1 Cut the steak into thin strips and place in a shallow dish.

2 Mix together the garlic, star anise, and dark soy sauce in a bowl and pour over the steak strips, turning them to coat thoroughly. Cover and leave to marinate in the refrigerator for at least 1 hour.

3 Heat the oil in a preheated wok. Reduce the heat, add the halved scallions and stir-fry for 1-2 minutes. Remove from the wok and set aside.

4 Add the beef to the wok, together with the marinade, and stir-fry for 3–4 minutes. Return the halved scallions to the wok and add the soy sauce, sherry, chili sauce, and two thirds of the water.

5 Blend the cornstarch to a paste with the remaining water and stir into the wok. Bring to a boil, stirring until the sauce thickens and clears.

6 Transfer to a warm serving dish, garnish with spring onion tassels and serve.

COOK'S TIP

Omit the chili sauce for a milder dish.

Egg Noodles with Beef

*Quick and easy, this mouth-watering Chinese-style
noodle dish can be cooked in minutes.*

Serves 4

INGREDIENTS

10 oz egg noodles
3 tbsp walnut oil
1 inch piece gingerroot, cut into thin
  strips
5 scallions, finely shredded
2 garlic cloves, finely chopped
1 red bell pepper, cored, seeded, and

thinly sliced
3$^{1}/_{2}$ oz button mushrooms, thinly
  sliced
12 oz steak tenderloin, cut into
  thin strips
1 tbsp cornstarch
5 tbsp dry sherry

3 tbsp soy sauce
1 tsp soft brown sugar
1 cup mung beansprouts
1 tbsp sesame oil
salt and pepper
scallion strips, to garnish

1 Bring a large saucepan of water to a boil. Add the noodles and cook according to the directions on the packet. Drain the noodles and set aside.

2 Heat the walnut oil in a preheated wok. Add the ginger, scallions, and garlic and stir-fry for 45 seconds. Add the bell pepper, mushrooms, and steak and stir-fry for 4 minutes. Season to taste with salt and pepper.

3 Mix together the cornstarch, sherry, and soy sauce in a small jug to form a paste, and pour into the wok. Sprinkle over the brown sugar and stir-fry all of the ingredients for a further 2 minutes.

4 Add the beansprouts, drained noodles, and sesame oil to the wok, stir and toss together for 1 minute. Garnish with strips of scallion and serve immediately.

COOK'S TIP

*If you do not have a wok, you could
prepare this dish in a skillet.
However, a wok is preferable, as
the round base ensures an even
distribution of heat and it is easier
to keep stirring and tossing the
contents when stir-frying.*

Creamed Strips of Sirloin with Rigatoni

*This quick and easy dish tastes superb and would
make a delicious treat for a special occasion.*

Serves 4

INGREDIENTS

6 tbsp butter
1 lb sirloin steak, trimmed and cut
 into thin strips
6 oz button mushrooms, sliced
1 tsp mustard
pinch of freshly grated gingerroot

2 tbsp dry sherry
5/8 cup heavy cream
salt and pepper
4 slices hot toast, cut into triangles,
 to serve

PASTA:
1 lb dried rigatoni
2 tbsp olive oil
2 fresh basil sprigs
8 tbsp butter

1 Preheat the oven to 375°F.
Melt the butter in a large
skillet and gently fry the steak over
a low heat, stirring frequently, for
6 minutes. Using a draining
spoon, transfer the steak to an
ovenproof dish and keep warm.

2 Add the sliced mushrooms to
the skillet and cook for 2–3
minutes in the juices remaining in
the pan. Add the mustard, ginger,
salt, and pepper. Cook for 2
minutes, then add the sherry and
cream. Cook for a further 3

minutes, then pour the cream
sauce over the steak.

3 Bake the steak and cream
mixture in the preheated oven
for 10 minutes.

4 Meanwhile, cook the pasta.
Bring a large saucepan of
lightly salted water to a boil. Add
the rigatoni, olive oil, and 1 of the
basil sprigs and boil rapidly for
10 minutes, until tender but still
firm to the bite. Drain the pasta
and transfer to a warm serving

plate. Toss the pasta with the
butter and garnish with a sprig
of basil.

5 Serve the steak with the pasta
and triangles of warm toast.

COOK'S TIP

*Dried pasta will keep for up to 6
months. Keep it in the packet and
reseal it once you have opened it, or
transfer the pasta to an airtight jar.*

Liver & Onion kabobs

Liver is full of iron, making this dish nutritious as well as flavorsome.

Makes 4

INGREDIENTS

12 oz lamb's liver
2 tbsp seasoned all-purpose flour
$\frac{1}{2}$ tsp dried mixed herbs
$4\frac{1}{2}$ oz rindless sliced bacon

2 medium onions
$2\frac{3}{4}$ oz butter
2 tsp balsamic vinegar

TO SERVE:
mixed salad leaves
tomato quarters

1 Cut the liver into bite-sized pieces. Mix the flour with the dried herbs and toss the liver in the seasoned flour.

2 Stretch out the bacon rashers with the back of a knife. Cut each rasher in half and wrap the bacon around half of the liver pieces.

3 Thread the plain liver pieces on to skewers, alternating with the bacon-wrapped liver pieces.

4 Cut the onions into rings and thread over the kabobs. Finely chop the onion rings that are too small to thread over the kabobs.

5 Heat the butter in a small pan and sauté the chopped onions for about 5 minutes until soft. Stir in the vinegar.

6 Brush the butter mixture over the kabobs and grill over hot coals for 8–10 minutes, basting occasionally with the butter mixture, until the liver is just cooked but is still a little pink inside.

7 Transfer the kabobs to serving plates. Serve with mixed salad leaves and tomatoes.

COOK'S TIP

Choose thick slices of liver to give good-sized pieces. Use bacon to hold 2–3 pieces of thinner liver together if necessary.

Fried Kidneys

*Fried lamb kidneys are a popular dish for a late breakfast or brunch,
served with Paratas and a fried egg.*

Serves 4

INGREDIENTS

1 lb lamb's kidneys
1 green bell pepper, sliced
²/₃ cup water
1 tsp fresh gingerroot, finely
  chopped

1 tsp fresh garlic, minced
1 tsp chili powder
¹/₂ tsp salt
3 tbsp oil

1 small onion, finely chopped
cilantro leaves, to garnish

1 Using a sharp knife, remove the very fine skin surrounding each kidney. Cut each kidney into 4-6 pieces.

2 Place the kidney pieces in a bowl of warm water with 2 teaspoons of turmeric and 2 teaspoons of salt for about 1 hour. Drain the kidneys thoroughly, then rinse them under cold running water until the water runs clear.

3 Place the kidneys in a small saucepan together with the green bell pepper. Pour in enough water to cover and cook over a medium heat, leaving the lid of the pan slightly ajar so that the steam can escape, until all of the water has evaporated.

4 Add the ginger, garlic, chili powder, and salt to the kidney mixture and blend until well combined.

5 Add the oil, onion, and the cilantro to the pan, and stir-fry for 7-10 minutes.

6 Transfer the kidneys to a serving plate and serve hot.

COOK'S TIP

Many people are resistant to the idea of cooking or eating kidneys because they often have rather a strong smell – even when cooked. However, if you wash and soak them in water, you can largely avoid this problem.

Spicy Peanut Chicken

This quick dish has many variations, but this version includes the classic combination of peanuts, chicken, and chilies, blending together to give a wonderfully flavored dish.

Serves 4

INGREDIENTS

10^1/$_2$ oz skinless, boneless chicken
  breast
2 tbsp peanut oil
1 cup shelled peanuts
1 fresh red chili, sliced
1 green bell pepper, seeded and cut
  into strips

fried rice, to serve

SAUCE:
^{2}/$_3$ cup chicken stock
1 tbsp Chinese rice wine or
  dry sherry
1 tbsp light soy sauce

1^1/$_2$ tsp light brown sugar
2 garlic cloves, minced
1 tsp grated fresh gingerroot
1 tsp rice-wine vinegar
1 tsp sesame oil

1 Trim any fat from the chicken and cut the meat into 1-inch cubes. Set aside.

2 Heat the peanut oil in a preheated wok. Add the peanuts and stir-fry for 1 minute. Remove the peanuts with a draining spoon and set aside.

3 Add the chicken to the wok and cook for 1–2 minutes. Stir in the chili and green bell pepper and cook for 1 minute.

Remove from the wok with a draining spoon and set aside.

4 Put half of the peanuts in a food processor and process until almost smooth. Alternatively, place them in a plastic bag and crush them with a rolling pin.

5 To make the sauce, add the chicken stock, Chinese rice wine or dry sherry, soy sauce, sugar, garlic, ginger, and rice-wine vinegar to the wok.

6 Heat the sauce without boiling and stir in the peanuts, chicken, chili, and bell pepper.

7 Sprinkle the sesame oil into the wok, stir and cook for 1 minute. Serve hot with fried rice.

COOK'S TIP

If necessary, process the peanuts with a little of the stock in step 4 to form a softer paste.

Lemon Chicken

This is on everyone's list of favorite Chinese dishes, and it is so simple to make. Fried chicken is cooked in a tangy lemon sauce in minutes and is great served with stir-fried vegetables.

Serves 4

INGREDIENTS

vegetable oil, for deep-frying
1¹/₂ lb skinless, boneless chicken, cut
   into strips
lemon slices and shredded scallion,
   to garnish

SAUCE:
1 tbsp cornstarch
6 tbsp cold water
3 tbsp fresh lemon juice

2 tbsp sweet sherry
¹/₂ tsp superfine sugar

1 Heat the oil in a preheated wok until almost smoking. Reduce the heat and stir-fry the chicken strips for 3–4 minutes, until cooked through. Remove the chicken with a draining spoon, set aside and keep warm. Drain the oil from the wok.

2 To make the sauce, mix the cornflour with 2 tablespoons of the water to form a paste.

3 Pour the lemon juice and remaining water into the mixture in the wok. Add the sherry and sugar and bring to a boil, stirring until the sugar has completely dissolved.

4 Stir in the cornstarch mixture and return to a boil. Reduce the heat and simmer, stirring constantly, for 2-3 minutes, until the sauce is thickened and clear.

5 Transfer the chicken to a warm serving plate and pour the sauce over the top. Garnish with the lemon slices and shredded scallion and serve immediately.

COOK'S TIP

If you would prefer to use chicken portions rather than strips, cook them in the oil, covered, over a low heat for about 30 minutes, or until cooked through.

Chili Chicken

This is quite a hot dish, using fresh chilies. If you prefer a milder dish, halve the number of chilies used.

Serves 4

INGREDIENTS

12 oz skinless, boneless
   lean chicken
$^1/_2$ tsp salt
1 egg white, lightly beaten
2 tbsp cornstarch
4 tbsp vegetable oil

2 garlic cloves, minced
$^1/_2$-inch piece gingerroot, grated
1 red bell pepper, seeded and diced
1 green bell pepper, seeded
   and diced
2 fresh red chilies, chopped

2 tbsp light soy sauce
1 tbsp dry sherry or Chinese rice wine
1 tbsp wine vinegar

1 Cut the chicken into cubes and place in a mixing bowl. Add the salt, egg white, cornstarch, and 1 tablespoon of the oil. Turn the chicken in the mixture to coat thoroughly.

2 Heat the remaining oil in a preheated wok. Add the garlic and ginger and stir-fry for 30 seconds.

3 Add the chicken pieces to the wok and stir-fry for 2–3 minutes, or until browned.

4 Stir in the bell peppers, chilies, soy sauce, sherry, or Chinese rice wine, and wine vinegar and cook for a further 2–3 minutes, until the chicken is cooked through. Transfer to a warm serving dish and serve.

VARIATION

This recipe works well if you use 12 oz lean steak, cut into thin strips or 1 lb raw shrimp instead of the chicken.

COOK'S TIP

When preparing chilies, wear rubber gloves to prevent the juices from burning and irritating your hands. Be careful not to touch your face, especially your lips or eyes until you have washed your hands.

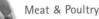

Chicken Chop Suey

Both well known and popular, chop suey dishes are easy to make and delicious.
They are based on beansprouts and soy sauce with a meat or vegetable flavoring.

Serves 4

INGREDIENTS

4 tbsp light soy sauce

2 tsp light brown sugar

1¹/₄ lb skinless, boneless chicken
   breasts

3 tbsp vegetable oil

2 onions, quartered

2 garlic cloves, minced

12 oz mung beansprouts

3 tsp sesame oil

1 tbsp cornstarch

3 tbsp water

2 cups chicken stock

shredded leek, to garnish

1 Mix the soy sauce and sugar
together, stirring until the
sugar has dissolved.

2 Trim any fat from the chicken
and cut the meat into thin
strips. Place the chicken strips in a
shallow glass dish and spoon the
soy mixture over them, turning
to coat. Leave to marinate in the
refrigerator for 20 minutes.

3 Heat the oil in a preheated
wok. Add the chicken and
stir-fry for 2–3 minutes, until
golden brown.

4 Add the onions and garlic and
cook for a further 2 minutes.
Add the beansprouts, cook for a
further 4–5 minutes, then add the
sesame oil.

5 Blend the cornstarch with the
water to form a smooth paste.
Pour the stock into the wok,
together with the cornflour paste
and bring to a boil, stirring
constantly until the sauce is
thickened and clear. Transfer to a
warm serving dish, garnish with
shredded leek, and serve.

VARIATION

This recipe may be made with
strips of lean steak, pork, or with
mixed vegetables. Change the type
of stock accordingly.

Tom's Toad in the Hole

This unusual recipe uses chicken and Cumberland sausage,
which is then made into individual bite-sized cakes.

Serves 4-6

INGREDIENTS

1 all-purpose flour	1 scant cup milk	9 oz chicken breasts
pinch of salt	$^1/_3$ cup water	9 oz Cumberland sausage
1 egg, beaten	2 tbsp beef drippings	

1 Mix the flour and salt in a bowl, make a well in the center, and add the beaten egg.

2 Add half the milk, and using a wooden spoon, work in the flour slowly.

3 Beat the mixture until smooth, then add the remaining milk and water.

4 Beat again until the mixture is smooth. Let the mixture stand for at least 1 hour.

5 Add the drippings to individual baking pans or to one large baking pan. Cut up the chicken and sausage so that you get a generous piece in each individual pan or several scattered around the large pan.

6 Heat in a preheated oven, 425°F, for 5 minutes until very hot. Remove the pans from the oven and pour in the batter, leaving space for the mixture to expand.

7 Return to the oven to cook for 35 minutes, until risen and golden brown. Do not open the oven door for at least 30 minutes.

8 Serve while hot, with chicken or onion gravy, or alone.

VARIATION

Use skinless, boneless chicken legs instead of chicken breast in the recipe. Cut up as directed. Instead of Cumberland sausage, use your favorite variety of sausage.

Golden Chicken Risotto

If you prefer, ordinary long grain rice can be used instead of risotto rice, but it will not give you the traditional, deliciously creamy texture that is typical of Italian risottos.

Serves 4

INGREDIENTS

2 tbsp sunflower oil
1 tbsp butter or margarine
1 medium leek, thinly sliced
1 large yellow bell pepper, diced
3 skinless, boneless chicken breasts, diced
12 oz arborio rice
few strands saffron
6 $^1/_4$ cups chicken stock

7 oz can corn

$^1/_2$ cup toasted unsalted peanuts

$^1/_2$ cup grated Parmesan cheese
salt and pepper

1 Heat the oil and butter or margarine in a large saucepan. Fry the leek and bell pepper for 1 minute then stir in the chicken and cook, stirring until golden brown.

2 Stir in the rice and cook for 2–3 minutes.

3 Stir in the saffron strands, and salt and pepper to taste.

Add the stock, a little at a time, cover and cook over a low heat, stirring occasionally, for about 20 minutes, until the rice is tender and most of the liquid is absorbed. Do not let the risotto dry out – add more stock if necessary.

4 Stir in the corn, peanuts, and Parmesan cheese, then adjust the seasoning to taste. Serve hot.

COOK'S TIP

Risottos can be frozen, before adding the Parmesan cheese, for up to 1 month, but remember to reheat this risotto thoroughly as it contains chicken.

Mediterranean Chicken Packets

This method of cooking makes the chicken aromatic and succulent. It also reduces the amount of oil needed since the chicken and vegetables cook in their own juices.

Serves 6

INGREDIENTS

1 tbsp olive oil
6 skinless chicken breast fillets
2 cups Mozzarella cheese

3^1/$_2$ cups zucchini, sliced
6 large tomatoes, sliced
1 small bunch fresh basil or oregano

pepper
rice or pasta, to serve

1 Cut six pieces of foil each about 10 inches square. Brush the foil squares lightly with oil and set aside until required.

2 With a sharp knife, slash each chicken breast at intervals, then slice the Mozzarella cheese and place between the cuts in the chicken.

3 Divide the zucchini and tomatoes between the pieces of foil and sprinkle with black pepper. Tear or roughly chop the basil or oregano and scatter over the vegetables in each packet.

4 Place the chicken on top of each pile of vegetables then wrap in the foil to enclose the chicken and vegetables, tucking in the ends.

5 Place on a baking sheet and bake in a preheated oven, 400°C, for about 30 minutes.

6 To serve, unwrap each foil parcel and serve with rice or pasta.

COOK'S TIP

To aid cooking, place the vegetables and chicken on the shiny side of the foil so that once the packet is wrapped up the dull surface of the foil is facing outwards. This ensures that the heat is absorbed into the packet and not reflected away from it.

Golden Glazed Chicken

A glossy glaze with sweet and fruity flavors coats chicken breasts in this tasty recipe.

Serves 6

INGREDIENTS

6 boneless chicken breasts
1 tsp turmeric
1 tbsp whole-grain mustard
1¹/₄ cups orange juice

2 tbsp clear honey
2 tbsp sunflower oil
1¹/₂ cups long grain rice
1 orange

3 tbsp chopped mint
salt and pepper
mint sprigs, to garnish

1 With a sharp knife, mark the surface of the chicken breasts in a diamond pattern. Mix together the turmeric, mustard, orange juice, and honey and pour over the chicken. Chill until required.

2 Lift the chicken from the marinade and pat dry on paper towels.

3 Heat the oil in a wide pan, add the chicken and sauté until golden, turning once. Drain off any excess oil. Pour over the marinade, cover and simmer for 10–15 minutes until the chicken is tender.

4 Boil the rice in lightly salted water until tender and drain well. Finely grate the rind from the orange and stir into the rice with the mint.

5 Using a sharp knife, remove the peel and white pith from the orange and cut the flesh into segments.

6 Serve the chicken with the orange and mint rice, garnished with orange segments and mint sprigs.

VARIATION

To make a slightly sharper sauce, use small grapefruit instead of the oranges.

Chicken Strips & Dips

Very simple to make and easy to eat with fingers, this dish can be served warm for a light lunch or cold as part of a buffet.

Serves 2

INGREDIENTS

2 boneless chicken breasts
2 tbsp all-purpose flour
1 tbsp sunflower oil

PEANUT DIP:
3 tbsp smooth or crunchy
   peanut butter
4 tbsp unsweetened yogurt
1 tsp grated orange rind
orange juice (optional)

TOMATO DIP:
5 tbsp creamy fromage blanc
1 medium tomato
2 tsp tomato paste
1 tsp chopped fresh chives

1 Using a sharp knife, slice the chicken into fairly thin strips and toss in the flour to coat.

2 Heat the oil in a non-stick skillet and fry the chicken until golden and thoroughly cooked. Remove the chicken strips from the skillet and drain well on absorbent paper towels.

3 To make the peanut dip, mix together all the ingredients in a bowl (if liked, add a little orange juice to thin the consistency).

4 To make the tomato dip, chop the tomato and mix with the remaining ingredients.

5 Serve the chicken strips with the dips and a selection of vegetable sticks for dipping.

VARIATION

For a lower-fat alternative, poach the strips of chicken in a small amount of boiling chicken stock for 6–8 minutes.

VARIATION

For a refreshing guacamole dip, combine 1 mashed avocado, 2 finely chopped scallions, 1 chopped tomato, 1 minced garlic clove and a squeeze of lemon juice. Remember to add the lemon juice immediately after the avocado has been mashed to prevent discoloration.

Deviled Chicken

Chicken is spiked with cayenne pepper and paprika and finished off with a fruity sauce.

Serves 2-3

INGREDIENTS

¹/₄ cup all-purpose flour
1 tbsp cayenne pepper
1 tsp paprika
12 oz skinless, boneless chicken, diced
2 tbsp butter

1 onion, chopped finely
2 cups milk, warmed
4 tbsp apple purée

³/₄ cup white grapes
²/₃ cup sour cream
sprinkle of paprika

1 Mix the flour, cayenne pepper, and paprika together and use to coat the chicken.

2 Shake off any excess flour. Melt the butter in a saucepan and gently fry the chicken with the onion for 4 minutes.

3 Stir in the flour and spice mixture. Add the milk slowly, stirring until the sauce thickens.

4 Simmer until the sauce is smooth.

5 Add the apple purée and grapes and simmer gently for 20 minutes.

6 Transfer the chicken and deviled sauce to a serving dish and top with sour cream and a sprinkle of paprika.

VARIATION

For a healthier alternative to soured cream, use unsweetened yogurt.

COOK'S TIP

Add more paprika if desired – as it is quite a mild spice, you can add plenty without it being too overpowering.

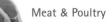

Speedy Peanut Pan-Fry

A complete main course cooked within ten minutes. Thread egg noodles are the ideal accompaniment because they can be cooked quickly and easily while the stir-fry sizzles.

Serves 4

INGREDIENTS

2 cups zucchini
1^1/$_3$ cups baby-corn-on-the-cobs
3^3/$_4$ cups button mushrooms
3 cups thread egg noodles
2 tbsp corn oil

1 tbsp sesame oil
8 boneless chicken thighs
   or 4 breasts, sliced thinly
1^1/$_2$ cups mung bean sprouts
4 tbsp smooth peanut butter

2 tbsp soy sauce
2 tbsp lime or lemon juice
^{1}/$_2$ cup roasted peanuts
pepper
cilantro, to garnish

1 Using a sharp knife, trim and thinly slice the zucchini, corn-on-the-cobs, and button mushrooms.

2 Bring a large pan of lightly salted boiling water to a boil and cook the noodles for 3–4 minutes. Meanwhile, heat the corn oil and sesame oil in a large skillet or wok and fry the chicken over a fairly high heat for 1 minute.

3 Add the sliced zucchini, corn-on-the-cobs, and button mushrooms and stir-fry for 5 minutes.

4 Add the bean sprouts, peanut butter, soy sauce, lime or lemon juice, and pepper, then cook for a further 2 minutes.

5 Drain the noodles, transfer to a serving dish, and scatter with the peanuts.

COOK'S TIP

Try serving this stir-fry with rice sticks. These are broad, pale, translucent ribbon noodles made from ground rice.

Steamed Chicken & Spring Vegetable Parcels

A healthy recipe with a delicate Oriental flavor, ideal for tender young summer vegetables.
You'll need large spinach leaves to wrap around the chicken, but make sure they are young leaves.

Serves 4

INGREDIENTS

4 boneless, skinless
  chicken breasts
1 tsp ground lemongrass
2 scallions,
  chopped finely
1 cup young carrots

$1^3/_4$ cups young zucchini
2 stalks celery
1 tsp light soy sauce
$^3/_4$ cup spinach leaves
2 tsp sesame oil
salt and pepper

1 With a sharp knife, make a slit through one side of each chicken breast, to open out a large pocket. Sprinkle the inside of the pocket with lemongrass, salt, and pepper. Tuck the scallions into the pockets.

2 Trim the carrots, zucchini, and celery and cut into small matchsticks. Plunge them into a pan of boiling water for 1 minute, drain and toss in the soy sauce.

3 Pack the vegetables into the pockets in each chicken breast and fold over firmly to enclose. Reserve any remaining vegetables. Wash the spinach leaves thoroughly, drain, and pat dry with paper towels. Wrap the chicken breasts firmly in the spinach leaves to enclose completely. If the leaves are too firm to wrap the chicken easily, steam them for a few seconds until they are softened and flexible.

4 Place the wrapped chicken in a steamer and steam over rapidly boiling water for 20–25 minutes, depending on size.

5 Stir-fry any leftover vegetable stalks and spinach for 1–2 minutes in the sesame oil and serve with the chicken.

Poached Breast of Chicken with Whiskey Sauce

*After cooking with stock and vegetables, chicken breasts are served
with a velvety sauce made from whiskey and crème fraîche.*

Serves 6

INGREDIENTS

2 tbsp butter
1/2 cup shredded leeks
1/3 cup diced carrot
1/4 cup diced celery
4 shallots, sliced

2 1/2 cups chicken stock
6 chicken breasts
1/4 cup whiskey
1 scant cup crème fraîche
2 tbsp freshly grated horseradish

1 tsp honey, warmed
1 tsp chopped fresh parsley
salt and pepper
sprig of fresh parsley, to garnish

1 Melt the butter in a large saucepan and add the leeks, carrot, celery, and shallots. Cook for 3 minutes, add half the chicken stock, and cook for about 8 minutes.

2 Add the remaining chicken stock, bring to a boil, add the chicken breasts, and cook for 10 minutes.

3 Remove the chicken and thinly slice. Place on a large, hot serving dish and keep warm until required.

4 In another saucepan, heat the whiskey until reduced by half. Strain the chicken stock through a fine sieve, add to the pan, and reduce the liquid by half.

5 Add the crème fraîche, the horseradish, and the honey. Heat gently and add the chopped parsley and salt and pepper to taste. Stir until well blended.

6 Pour a little of the whiskey sauce around the chicken and pour the remaining sauce into a sauceboat to serve.

7 Serve with a vegetable patty made from the leftover vegetables, mashed potato, and fresh vegetables. Garnish with the parsley sprig.

Chicken with Two bell Pepper Sauce

This quick and simple dish is colorful and healthy.
It would be perfect for an impromptu lunch or supper dish.

Serves 4

INGREDIENTS

2 tbsp olive oil
2 medium onions, chopped finely
2 garlic cloves, minced
2 red bell peppers, chopped
good pinch cayenne pepper
2 tsp tomato paste

2 yellow bell peppers, chopped
pinch of dried basil
4 skinless, boneless
  chicken breasts
$2/3$ cup dry white wine
$2/3$ cup chicken stock

bouquet garni
salt and pepper
fresh herbs, to garnish

1 Heat 1 tablespoon of oil in each of two medium-sized saucepans. Place half the chopped onions, 1 of the garlic cloves, the red bell peppers, the cayenne pepper, and the tomato paste in one of the saucepans. Place the remaining onion, garlic, yellow bell peppers, and basil in the other pan.

2 Cover each pan and cook over a very low heat for 1 hour until the bell peppers are soft. If either mixture becomes

dry, add a little water. Work each mixture separately in a food processor, then sieve separately.

3 Return the separate mixtures to the pans and season. The two sauces can be gently re-heated while the chicken is cooking.

4 Put the chicken breasts into a skillet and add the wine and stock. Add the bouquet garni and bring the liquid to simmer. Cook the chicken for about 20 minutes until tender.

5 To serve, pour a serving of each sauce on to four serving plates, slice the chicken breasts, and arrange on the plates. Garnish with fresh herbs.

COOK'S TIP

Make your own bouquet garni by tying together sprigs of your favorite herbs with string, or wrap up dried herbs in a piece of muslin. A popular combination is thyme, parsley, and bay.

Chicken Risotto alla Milanese

This famous dish is known throughout the world, and it is perhaps the best known of all Italian risottos, although there are many variations.

Serves 4

INGREDIENTS

¹/₂ cup butter
2 lb chicken meat, sliced thinly
1 large onion, chopped
2¹/₂ cups risotto rice
2¹/₂ cups chicken stock

²/₃ cup white wine
1 tsp crumbled saffron
salt and pepper
¹/₂ cup grated
    Parmesan cheese, to serve

1 Heat 4 tbsp of butter in a deep skillet and fry the chicken and onion until golden brown.

2 Add the rice, stir well, and cook for 15 minutes.

3 Heat the stock until boiling and gradually add to the rice. Add the white wine, saffron, salt, and pepper to taste and mix well. Simmer gently for 20 minutes, stirring occasionally, and adding more stock if the risotto becomes too dry.

4 Leave to stand for a few minutes and just before serving add a little more stock and simmer for a further 10 minutes. Serve the risotto, sprinkled with the grated Parmesan cheese and the remaining butter.

COOK'S TIP

A risotto should have moist but separate grains. Stock should be added a little at a time and only when the last addition has been completely absorbed.

VARIATION

The possibilities for risotto are endless – try adding the following just at the end of cooking time: cashew nuts and corn, lightly sautéed zucchini and basil, or artichokes and oyster mushrooms.

Harlequin Chicken

This colorful, simple dish will tempt the appetites of all the family – it is ideal for toddlers, who enjoy the fun shapes of the multi-colored bell peppers.

Serves 4

INGREDIENTS

10 skinless, boneless chicken thighs
1 medium onion
1 each medium red, green,
   and yellow bell peppers
1 tbsp sunflower oil

14 oz can chopped tomatoes
2 tbsp chopped fresh parsley
pepper
whole-wheat bread and a green
   salad, to serve

1 Using a sharp knife, cut the chicken thighs into bite-sized pieces.

2 Peel and thinly slice the onion. Halve and seed the bell peppers and cut into small diamond shapes.

3 Heat the oil in a shallow skillet. Add the chicken and onion and fry quickly until golden.

4 Add the bell peppers, cook for 2–3 minutes, stir in the tomatoes and parsley, and season with pepper.

5 Cover tightly and simmer for about 15 minutes, until the chicken and vegetables are tender. Serve hot with whole-wheat bread and a green salad.

COOK'S TIP

You can use dried parsley instead of fresh, but remember that you only need about one half of dried to fresh.

COOK'S TIP

If you are making this dish for small children, the chicken can be finely chopped or ground first.

Elizabethan Chicken

Chicken is surprisingly delicious when combined
with fruits such as grapes or gooseberries.

Serves 4

INGREDIENTS

1 tbsp butter

1 tbsp sunflower oil

4 skinless, boneless
chicken breasts

4 shallots, finely chopped

$^2/_3$ cup chicken stock

1 tbsp cider vinegar

1 cup halved
seedless grapes

$^1/_2$ cup heavy cream

1 tsp freshly grated nutmeg

cornstarch, to thicken,
(optional)

salt and pepper

---

1 Heat the butter and sunflower oil in a wide, flameproof casserole or tin and quickly fry the chicken breasts until golden brown, turning once. Remove the chicken breasts and keep warm while you are cooking the shallots.

2 Add the chopped shallots to the pan and fry gently until softened and lightly browned. Return the chicken breasts to the pan.

3 Add the chicken stock and cider vinegar to the pan, bring to a boil, cover, and simmer gently for 10–12 minutes, stirring occasionally.

4 Transfer the chicken to a serving dish. Add the grapes, cream, and nutmeg to the pan. Heat through, seasoning with salt and pepper to taste. Add a little cornstarch to thicken the sauce, if desired. Pour the sauce over the chicken and serve.

VARIATION

If desired, add a little dry white
wine or vermouth to the sauce
in step 3.

Quick Chicken Bake

This recipe is a type of pie and is very versatile. Add vegetables and herbs of your choice, depending on what you have at hand.

Serves 4

INGREDIENTS

1 lb 2 oz ground chicken
1 large onion, chopped finely
2 carrots, diced finely
2 tbsp all-purpose flour
1 tbsp tomato paste

1$^1/_4$ cups chicken stock
pinch of fresh thyme
2 lb potatoes, creamed with butter
   and milk and highly seasoned
$^3/_4$ cup grated hard cheese
salt and pepper
peas, to serve

1 Dry-fry the ground chicken, onion, and carrots in a non-stick saucepan for 5 minutes, stirring frequently.

2 Sprinkle the chicken with the flour and simmer for a further 2 minutes.

3 Gradually blend in the tomato paste and stock then simmer for 15 minutes. Season and add the thyme.

4 Transfer the chicken and vegetable mixture to a baking casserole and allow to cool.

5 Spoon the mashed potato over the chicken mixture and sprinkle with the hard cheese. Bake in a preheated oven at 400°F for 20 minutes, or until the cheese is bubbling and golden, then serve with the peas.

VARIATION

Instead of hard cheese, you could sprinkle any cheese of your choice over the top of the pie. Choose a cheese which melts easily to use as a topping. Alternatively, you could use a mixture of cheeses, depending on whatever you have at hand.

Sliced Breast of Duck with Linguine

A raspberry and honey sauce superbly counterbalances the richness of the duck.

Serves 4

INGREDIENTS

10¹/₂ oz boned breasts
   of duck
2 tbsp butter
³/₈ cup finely chopped carrots
4 tbsp finely chopped shallots
1 tbsp lemon juice
⁵/₈ cup meat stock
4 tbsp honey

³/₄ cup fresh or thawed frozen
   raspberries
¹/₄ cup all-purpose flour
1 tbsp Worcestershire sauce
14 oz fresh linguine
1 tbsp olive oil
salt and pepper

TO GARNISH:
fresh raspberries
fresh sprig of flat-leaf parsley

1 Trim and score the duck breasts with a sharp knife and season well all over. Melt the butter in a skillet, add the duck breasts, and fry all over until lightly colored.

2 Add the carrots, shallots, lemon juice, and half the meat stock and simmer over a low heat for 1 minute. Stir in half the honey and half the raspberries. Sprinkle over half the flour and cook, stirring constantly for

3 minutes. Season with pepper and add the Worcestershire sauce.

3 Stir in the remaining stock and cook for 1 minute. Stir in the remaining honey and remaining raspberries and sprinkle over the remaining flour. Cook for a further 3 minutes.

4 Remove the duck breasts from the pan, but leave the sauce to continue simmering over a very low heat.

5 Meanwhile, bring a large saucepan of lightly salted water to a boil. Add the linguine and olive oil and cook until tender, but still firm to the bite. Drain and divide between 4 individual plates.

6 Slice the duck breast lengthways into ¹/₄ inch thick pieces. Pour a little sauce over the pasta and arrange the sliced duck in a fan shape on top of it. Garnish with raspberries and flat-leaf parsley and serve.

Honey-glazed Duck

This honey and soy glaze gives a wonderful sheen and flavor to the duck skin.
This is such a simple recipe, yet the result is unutterably delicious.

Serves 4

INGREDIENTS

1 tsp dark soy sauce
2 tbsp honey
1 tsp garlic vinegar
2 garlic cloves, minced

1 tsp ground star anise
2 tsp cornstarch
2 tsp water

2 large boneless duck breasts, about
  8 oz each
celery leaves, cucumber wedges, and
  snipped chives, to garnish

1 Mix together the soy sauce, clear honey, garlic vinegar, garlic, and star anise. Blend the cornstarch with the water to form a smooth paste and stir it into the mixture.

2 Place the duck breasts in a shallow ovenproof dish. Brush with the soy marinade, turning to coat them completely. Cover and leave to marinate in the refrigerator for at least 2 hours, or overnight if possible.

3 Remove the duck from the marinade and cook in a preheated oven, at 425°F for 20–25 minutes, basting frequently with the glaze.

4 Remove the duck from the oven and transfer to a preheated broiler. Broil for about 3–4 minutes to caramelize the top.

5 Remove the duck from the broiler pan and cut into thin slices. Arrange the duck slices in a warm serving dish, garnish with celery leaves, cucumber wedges, and snipped chives, and serve immediately.

COOK'S TIP

If the duck begins to burn slightly while it is cooking in the oven, cover with foil. Check that the duck breasts are cooked through by inserting the point of a sharp knife into the thickest part of the flesh – the juices should run clear.

Duck with Baby Corn & Pineapple

*The pineapple and plum sauce add a sweetness and fruity flavor
to this colorful recipe which blend well with the duck.*

Serves 4

INGREDIENTS

4 duck breasts	8 oz baby onions, peeled	1 cup beansprouts
1 tsp Chinese five spice powder	2 cloves garlic, minced	2 tbsp plum sauce
1 tbsp cornstarch	1 cup baby-corn-on-the-cobs	
1 tbsp chili oil	1¼ cups canned pineapple chunks	
	6 scallions, sliced	

1 Remove any skin from the duck breasts. Cut the duck breasts into thin slices.

2 Mix together the five spice powder and the cornstarch in a large bowl.

3 Toss the duck in the five spice powder and cornstarch mixture until well coated.

4 Heat the oil in a preheated wok. Stir-fry the duck for 10 minutes, or until just beginning to crispen around the edges.

5 Remove the duck from the wok and set aside until required.

6 Add the onions and garlic to the wok and stir-fry for 5 minutes, or until the onions have softened.

7 Add the baby-corn-on-the-cobs to the wok and stir-fry for a further 5 minutes.

8 Add the pineapple, scallions, and beansprouts and stir-fry for 3–4 minutes. Stir in the plum sauce.

9 Return the cooked duck to the wok and toss until well mixed. Transfer to warm serving dishes and serve hot.

COOK'S TIP

Buy pineapple chunks in natural juice rather than syrup for a fresher flavor. If you can only obtain pineapple in syrup, rinse it in cold water and drain thoroughly before using.

Stir-Fried Turkey with Cranberry Glaze

This dish encompasses all of the flavors of Christmas with a Chinese theme! Turkey, cranberries, ginger, chestnuts, and soy sauce all blend perfectly in this quick stir-fry.

Serves 2–3

INGREDIENTS

1 turkey breast
2 tbsp sunflower oil
2 tbsp gingerroot

$^1/_2$ cup fresh or frozen cranberries
$^1/_4$ cup canned chestnuts
4 tbsp cranberry sauce

3 tbsp light soy sauce
salt and pepper

1 Remove any skin from the turkey breast. Using a sharp knife, thinly slice the turkey breast.

2 Heat the oil in a large preheated wok.

3 Add the turkey to the wok and stir-fry for 5 minutes, or until cooked through.

4 Using a sharp knife, finely chop the ginger.

5 Add the ginger and the cranberries to the wok and stir-fry for 2–3 minutes or until the cranberries have softened.

6 Add the chestnuts, cranberry sauce, and soy sauce, season to taste with salt and pepper, and allow to bubble for 2–3 minutes.

7 Transfer to warm serving dishes and serve immediately.

COOK'S TIP

If you wish, use a turkey escalope instead of the breast for really tender, lean meat.

COOK'S TIP

It is very important that the wok is very hot before you stir-fry. Test by by holding your hand flat about 3 inches above the base of the interior – you should be able to feel the heat radiating from it.

Fish & Seafood

The wealth of species and flavors that the world's oceans and rivers provide is immense. Each country combines its local catch with the region's favorite herbs and spices to create a variety of dishes. All of the recipes featured here are easy to prepare and delicious to eat. Moreover, not only are fish and seafood are quick to cook but they are packed full with nutritional goodness. Naturally low in fat, yet rich in minerals and proteins, fish and seafood are important to help balance any diet.

The superb recipes in this chapter demonstrate the richness of cooking with fish and seafood. Dishes include modern variations of traditional recipes, such as Sea Bass in Olive Sauce on a Bed of Macaroni and Potato-Topped Cod, and exotic flavors such as Caribbean Shrimp and Terriyaki Stir-Fried Salmon with Crispy Leeks. The variety of different fish and the prices of fish and seafood allow you to choose a dish to suit your mood and your pocket.

Caribbean Shrimp

This is an ideal recipe for cooks who have difficulty in finding raw shrimp.

Serves 4

INGREDIENTS

16 cooked tiger shrimp
1 small pineapple
flaked coconut, to garnish (optional)

MARINADE:
$2/3$ cup pineapple juice
2 tbsp white wine vinegar

2 tbsp dark muscovado sugar
2 tbsp shredded coconut

1 If they are unpeeled, peel the shrimp, leaving the tails attached if preferred.

2 Peel the pineapple and cut it in half lengthwise. Cut one pineapple half into wedges then into chunks.

3 To make the marinade, mix together half of the pineapple juice and the vinegar, sugar, and coconut in a shallow, nonmetallic dish. Add the peeled shrimp and pineapple chunks and toss until well coated. Leave the shrimp and pineapple to marinate for at least 30 minutes.

4 Remove the pineapple and shrimp from the marinade and thread them on to skewers. Reserve the marinade.

5 Strain the marinade and place in a food processor. Roughly chop the remaining pineapple and add to the processor with the remaining pineapple juice. Process the pineapple for a few seconds to produce a thick sauce.

6 Pour the sauce into a small saucepan. Bring to the boil, then simmer for about 5 minutes. This can be done by the side of the grill, if preferred.

7 Transfer the kabobs to the grill and brush with some of the sauce. Grill for about 5 minutes until the kabobs piping hot. Turn the kabobs, brushing occasionally with the sauce. Serve with extra sauce, sprinkled with flaked coconut (if using), on the side.

COOK'S TIP

Grill these kabobs just long enough to heat thorough. If cooked for too long, the shrimp will toughen.

Herb & Garlic Shrimp

*Look for raw shrimp in the freezer compartment
of large supermarkets or Oriental food stores.*

Serves 4

INGREDIENTS

12 oz raw shrimp, peeled

2 tbsp chopped, fresh parsley

4 tbsp lemon juice

2 tbsp olive oil

2¼ oz butter

2 cloves garlic, minced

salt and pepper

1 Place the prepared shrimp in a shallow, non-metallic dish with the parsley, lemon juice and salt and pepper to taste. Leave the shrimp to marinate in the herb mixture for at least 30 minutes.

2 Heat the oil and butter in a small pan with the garlic until the butter melts. Stir to mix well.

3 Remove the shrimp from the marinade with a draining spoon and add them to the pan containing the garlic butter. Stir the shrimp into the garlic butter until well coated, then thread the shrimp on to skewers.

4 Grill the kabobs over hot coals for 5–10 minutes, turning the skewers occasionally, until the shrimp turn pink and are cooked through. Brush the shrimp with the remaining garlic butter during the cooking time.

5 Transfer the herb and garlic shrimp kabobs to serving plates. Drizzle over any of the remaining garlic butter and serve at once.

VARIATION

If raw shrimp are unavailable, use cooked shrimp but reduce the cooking time. Small cooked shrimp can also be cooked in a kitchen foil parcel instead of on the skewers. Marinate and toss the cooked shrimp in the garlic butter, wrap in a kitchen foil, and cook for about 5 minutes, shaking the parcels once or twice.

Shrimp with Bell Peppers

This is a colorful and impressive side dish for a dinner party. As there are not many spices in this recipe, I like to use a lot of fresh cilantro in it.

Serves 4

INGREDIENTS

1 lb frozen shrimp	1 medium green bell pepper, sliced
$^1/_2$ bunch fresh cilantro leaves	
1 tsp fresh garlic, minced	1 medium red bell pepper
1 tsp salt	$5^1/_2$ tbsp unsalted butter

1 Defrost the shrimp and rinse under cold running water twice. Drain the shrimp thoroughly and place in a large mixing bowl.

2 Using a sharp knife, finely chop the bunch of fresh cilantro.

3 Add the garlic, salt, and fresh cilantro leaves to the shrimp and set aside until required.

4 Seed the bell peppers and cut into thin slices, using a sharp knife.

5 Melt the butter in a large skillet. Add the shrimp to the pan and stir-fry, stirring and tossing the shrimp gently, for 10-12 minutes.

6 Add the bell peppers to the pan and fry for a further 3-5 minutes, stirring occasionally.

7 Transfer the shrimp and bell pepper to a serving dish and serve hot.

VARIATION

You could use large tiger shrimp in this dish, if you prefer.

Shrimp with Tomatoes

Quick and easy to prepare, this dish is also extremely good to eat. Use the larger tiger shrimp for special occasions, if you prefer.

Serves 4–6

INGREDIENTS

3 medium onions
1 green bell pepper
1 tsp fresh gingerroot, finely minced

1 tsp fresh garlic, crushed
1 tsp salt
1 tsp chili powder
2 tbsp lemon juice

12 oz frozen shrimp
3 tbsp oil
14 oz can tomatoes
fresh cilantro leaves,
    to decorate

1 Using a sharp knife, slice the onions and the green bell pepper.

2 Place the ginger, garlic, salt, and chili powder in a small bowl and mix to combine. Add the lemon juice and mix to form a paste.

3 Place the shrimp in a bowl of cold water and set aside to defrost. Drain thoroughly.

4 Heat the oil in a medium-sized saucepan. Add the onions and fry until golden brown.

5 Add the spice paste to the onions, reduce the heat to low, and cook, stirring and mixing well, for about 3 minutes.

6 Add the tomatoes, tomato juice, and the green bell pepper, and cook for 5-7 minutes, stirring occasionally.

7 Add the shrimp to the pan and cook for 10 minutes, stirring occasionally. Garnish with fresh cilantro leaves and serve hot with plain boiled rice and a crisp green salad.

COOK'S TIP

Fresh gingerroot looks rather like a knobbly potato. The skin should be peeled, then the flesh either grated, finely minced, or sliced. Ginger is also available ground: this can be used as a substitute for fresh gingerroot, but the fresh root is far superior.

Shrimp with Spicy Tomatoes

Basil and tomatoes are ideal flavorings for shrimp spiced with cumin seeds and garlic.

Serves 4

INGREDIENTS

2 tbsp corn oil
1 onion
2 cloves garlic, minced
1 tsp cumin seeds

1 tbsp demerara sugar
14 oz can chopped tomatoes
1 tbsp sundried tomato paste
1 tbsp chopped fresh basil

1 lb peeled king shrimp
salt and pepper

1 Heat the corn oil in a large preheated wok.

2 Using a sharp knife, finely chop the onion.

3 Add the onion and garlic to the wok and stir-fry for 2–3 minutes, or until softened.

4 Stir in the cumin seeds and stir-fry for 1 minute.

5 Add the sugar, chopped tomatoes, and sundried tomato paste to the wok. Bring the mixture to the boil, reduce the heat, and leave the sauce to simmer for 10 minutes.

6 Add the basil, shrimp, and salt and pepper to taste to the mixture in the wok. Increase the heat and cook for a further 2–3 minutes or until the shrimp are completely cooked through.

COOK'S TIP

Always heat your wok before you add oil or other ingredients. This will prevent anything from sticking to it.

COOK'S TIP

Sundried tomato paste has a much more intense flavor than that of normal tomato paste. It adds a distinctive intensity to any tomato-based dish.

Shrimp Omelet

*This really is a meal in minutes, combining many
Chinese ingredients for a truly tasty dish.*

Serves 4

INGREDIENTS

2 tbsp sunflower oil	1 cup beansprouts	6 eggs
4 scallions, sliced	1 tsp cornstarch	
12 oz peeled shrimp	1 tbsp light soy sauce	

1 Heat the sunflower oil in a large preheated wok.

2 Using a sharp knife, trim the scallions, and cut into slices.

3 Add the shrimp, scallions, and beansprouts to the wok and stir-fry for 2 minutes.

4 Mix together the cornstarch and soy sauce in a small bowl.

5 Beat the eggs with 3 tablespoons of cold water and then blend with the cornstarch and soy mixture.

6 Add the egg mixture to the wok and cook for 5–6 minutes, or until the mixture sets.

7 Transfer the omelet to a serving plate and cut into quarters to serve.

COOK'S TIP

It is important to use fresh beansprouts for this dish as the canned ones don't have the crunchy texture necessary.

VARIATION

Add any other vegetables of your choice, such as grated carrot or cooked peas, to the omelet in step 3, if you wish.

Cantonese Shrimp

*This shrimp dish is very simple and is ideal
for supper or lunch when time is short.*

Serves 4

INGREDIENTS

5 tbsp vegetable oil

4 garlic cloves, crushed

1¹/₂ lb raw shrimp, shelled and
  deveined

2-inch piece fresh gingerroot, minced

6 oz lean pork, diced

1 leek, sliced

3 eggs, beaten

shredded leek and red bell pepper
  matchsticks, to garnish

SAUCE:

2 tbsp dry sherry

2 tbsp light soy sauce

2 tsp superfine sugar

²/₃ cup fish stock

4¹/₂ tsp cornstarch

3 tbsp water

1 Heat 2 tablespoons of the oil in a preheated wok. Add the garlic and stir-fry for 30 seconds. Add the shrimp and stir-fry for 5 minutes, or until they change color. Remove the shrimp from the wok with a draining spoon, set aside, and keep warm.

2 Add the remaining oil to the wok and heat. Add the ginger, diced pork, and leek and stir-fry over a medium heat for 4-5 minutes, or until the pork is lightly colored and sealed.

3 Add the sherry, soy sauce, sugar, and fish stock to the wok. Blend the cornstarch with the water to form a smooth paste and stir it into the wok. Cook, stirring, until the sauce thickens and clears.

4 Return the shrimp to the wok and add the beaten eggs. Cook for 5–6 minutes, gently stirring occasionally, until the eggs set. Transfer to a warm serving dish, garnish with shredded leek and bell pepper matchsticks, and serve immediately.

COOK'S TIP

*If possible, use Chinese rice wine
instead of the sherry.*

Fried Shrimp with Cashews

Cashew nuts are delicious as part of a stir-fry with almost any other ingredient.
Use the unsalted variety in cooking.

Serves 4

INGREDIENTS

2 garlic cloves, crushed
1 tbsp cornstarch
pinch of superfine sugar
1 lb raw tiger shrimp
4 tbsp vegetable oil
1 leek, sliced

$4^{1}/_{2}$ oz broccoli florets
1 orange bell pepper, seeded
  and diced
$^{3}/_{4}$ cup unsalted cashew nuts

SAUCE:
$^{3}/_{4}$ cup fish stock
1 tbsp cornstarch
dash of chili sauce
2 tsp sesame oil
1 tbsp Chinese rice wine

1 Mix together the garlic, cornstarch, and sugar in a bowl. Peel and devein the shrimp. Stir the shrimp into the mixture to coat thoroughly.

2 Heat the oil in a preheated wok and add the shrimp mixture. Stir-fry over a high heat for 20–30 seconds until the shrimp turn pink. Remove the shrimp from the wok with a draining spoon and set aside.

3 Add the leek, broccoli, and bell pepper to the wok and stir-fry for 2 minutes.

4 To make the sauce, mix together the fish stock, cornstarch, chili sauce to taste, the sesame oil, and Chinese rice wine. Add the mixture to the wok, together with the cashew nuts. Return the shrimp to the wok and cook for 1 minute to heat through. Transfer to a warm serving dish and serve immediately.

VARIATION

This recipe also works well with chicken, pork, or beef strips instead of the shrimp.
Use 8 oz meat instead of 1 lb shrimp.

Macaroni & Shrimp Bake

*This adaptation of an eighteenth-century Italian dish is baked until
it is golden brown and sizzling, then cut into wedges like a cake.*

Serves 4

INGREDIENTS

3 cups dried short-cut macaroni

1 tbsp olive oil, plus extra
   for brushing

6 tbsp butter, plus extra
   for greasing

2 small fennel bulbs, thinly sliced and
   fronds reserved

6 oz mushrooms, thinly sliced

6 oz peeled, cooked shrimp

pinch of cayenne pepper

1¼ cups Béchamel Sauce (see Cook's
   Tip, below)

²/₃ cup freshly grated Parmesan
   cheese

2 large tomatoes, sliced

1 tsp dried oregano

salt and pepper

---

1 Bring a saucepan of salted
water to the boil. Add the
pasta and oil and cook until
tender, but still firm to the bite.
Drain and return to the pan. Add
2 tbsp of butter, cover, shake the
pan, and keep warm.

2 Melt the remaining butter in
a saucepan. Fry the fennel for
3–4 minutes. Stir in the mushrooms
and fry for a further 2 minutes.
Stir in the shrimp, then remove
the pan from the heat.

3 Stir the cayenne pepper and
shrimp mixture into the
Béchamel sauce. Pour into a
greased ovenproof dish and spread
evenly. Sprinkle over the Parmesan
cheese and arrange the tomato
slices in a ring around the edge.
Brush the tomatoes with olive oil
and sprinkle over the oregano.

4 Cook in a preheated oven at
350°F for 25 minutes, until
golden brown. Serve immediately.

COOK'S TIP

*For Béchamel sauce, melt 2 tbsp
butter. Stir in ¼ cup flour. Cook,
stirring, for 2 minutes. Gradually,
stir in 1¼ cups warm milk. Add 2
tbsp finely minced onion, 5 white
peppercorns, and 2 parsley sprigs
and season with salt, dried thyme,
and grated nutmeg. Simmer,
stirring, for 15 minutes. Strain
before using.*

Mussel Casserole

Mussels are not difficult to cook, just a little messy to eat. The flavors are worth it, however, and serving this dish with a finger bowl helps to keep things clean!

Serves 4

INGREDIENTS

2 lb 4 oz mussels	1 onion, finely minced	3$^{1}/_{2}$ oz tomato paste
$^{2}/_{3}$ cup white wine	3 garlic cloves, minced	1 tbsp chopped marjoram
1 tbsp oil	1 red chili, finely minced	toast or crusty bread, to serve

1 Scrub the mussels to remove any mud or sand.

2 Remove the beards from the mussels by pulling away the hairy bit between the two shells. Rinse the mussels in a bowl of clean water. Discard any mussels that do not close when they are tapped – they are dead and should not be eaten.

3 Place the mussels in a large saucepan. Pour in the wine and cook for 5 minutes, shaking the pan occasionally until the shells open. Remove and discard any mussels that do not open.

4 Remove the mussels from the saucepan with a draining spoon. Strain the cooking liquid through a fine sifter set over a bowl, reserving the liquid.

5 Heat the oil in a large skillet. Add the onion, garlic, and chili and cook for 4–5 minutes or until softened.

6 Add the reserved cooking liquid to the pan and cook for 5 minutes or until reduced.

7 Stir in the tomato paste, marjoram, and mussels and cook until hot.

8 Transfer to serving bowls and serve with toast or plenty of crusty bread to mop up the juices.

COOK'S TIP

Finger bowls are individual bowls of warm water with a slice of lemon floating in them. They are used to clean your fingers at the end of a meal.

Pasta Shells with Mussels

Serve this aromatic seafood dish to family and friends who admit to a love of garlic.

Serves 4–6

INGREDIENTS

$2^3/_4$ lb mussels
1 cup dry white wine
2 large onions, minced
$^1/_2$ cup unsalted butter

6 large garlic cloves, finely minced
5 tbsp chopped fresh parsley
$1^1/_4$ cups heavy cream
14 oz dried pasta shells

1 tbsp olive oil
salt and pepper
crusty bread, to serve

1 Scrub and debeard the mussels under cold running water. Discard any that do not close immediately when sharply tapped. Put the mussels into a large saucepan, together with the wine and half of the onions. Cover and cook over a medium heat, shaking the pan frequently, for 2–3 minutes, until the shells open.

2 Remove the pan from the heat. Drain the mussels and reserve the cooking liquid. Discard any mussels that have not opened. Strain the cooking liquid through a clean cloth into a glass pitcher or bowl and reserve.

3 Melt the butter in a pan over a medium heat. Add the remaining onion and fry until translucent. Stir in the garlic and cook for 1 minute. Gradually stir in the reserved cooking liquid. Stir in the parsley and cream and season to taste with salt and black pepper. Bring to simmering point over a low heat.

4 Meanwhile, bring a large saucepan of lightly salted water to the boil. Add the pasta and olive oil and cook until just tender, but still firm to the bite. Drain the pasta, return to the pan, cover, and keep warm.

5 Reserve a few mussels for the garnish and remove the remainder from their shells. Stir the shelled mussels into the cream sauce and warm briefly.

6 Transfer the pasta to a large, warm serving dish. Pour over the sauce and toss well to coat. Garnish with the reserved mussels and serve with warm, crusty bread.

COOK'S TIP

Pasta shells are ideal because the sauce collects in the cavities and impregnates the pasta with flavor.

Saffron Mussel Tagliatelle

*Saffron is the most expensive spice in the world, but you only ever need
a small quantity. Saffron threads or powdered saffron may be used in this recipe.*

Serves 4

INGREDIENTS

$2^1/_4$ lb mussels	$1^1/_4$ cups heavy cream	1 tbsp olive oil
$5/_8$ cup white wine	pinch of saffron threads or	salt and pepper
1 medium onion, finely minced	saffron powder	3 tbsp chopped fresh parsley,
2 tbsp butter	juice of $1/_2$ lemon	to garnish
2 garlic cloves, crushed	1 egg yolk	
2 tsp cornstarch	1 lb dried tagliatelle	

1 Scrub and debeard the mussels under cold running water. Discard any that do not close when sharply tapped. Put the mussels in a pan with the wine and onion. Cover and cook over a high heat, shaking the pan, for 5–8 minutes, until the shells open.

2 Drain and reserve the cooking liquid. Discard any mussels that are still closed. Reserve a few mussels for the garnish and remove the remainder from their shells.

3 Strain the cooking liquid into a saucepan. Bring to the boil and reduce by about half. Remove the pan from the heat.

4 Melt the butter in a saucepan. Add the garlic and cook, stirring frequently, for 2 minutes, until golden brown. Stir in the cornstarch and cook, stirring, for 1 minute. Gradually stir in the cooking liquid and the cream. Crush the saffron threads and add to the pan. Season with salt and pepper to taste and simmer over a

low heat for 2–3 minutes, until thickened.

5 Stir in the egg yolk, lemon juice, and shelled mussels. Do not allow the mixture to boil.

6 Meanwhile, bring a pan of salted water to the boil. Add the pasta and oil and cook until tender, but still firm to the bite. Drain and transfer to a serving dish. Add the mussel sauce and toss. Garnish with the parsley and reserved mussels and serve.

Vermicelli with Clams

A quickly cooked recipe that transforms store-cupboard ingredients into a dish with style.

Serves 4

INGREDIENTS

14 oz dried vermicelli, spaghetti or
    other long pasta
2 tbsp olive oil
2 tbsp butter
2 onions, minced

2 garlic cloves, minced
2 x 7 oz jars clams in brine
1/2 cup white wine
4 tbsp chopped fresh parsley
1/2 tsp dried oregano

pinch of freshly grated nutmeg
salt and pepper

TO GARNISH:
2 tbsp Parmesan cheese shavings
fresh basil sprigs

---

1 Bring a large pan of lightly salted water to the boil. Add the pasta and half the olive oil and cook until tender, but still firm to the bite. Drain, return to the pan, and add the butter. Cover the pan, shake well and keep warm.

2 Heat the remaining oil in a pan over a medium heat. Add the onions and fry until they are translucent. Stir in the garlic and cook for 1 minute.

3 Strain the liquid from 1 jar of clams and add the liquid to the pan, with the wine. Stir, bring to simmering point, and simmer for 3 minutes. Drain the second jar of clams and discard the liquid.

4 Add the clams, parsley, and oregano to the pan and season with pepper and nutmeg. Lower the heat and cook until the sauce is heated through.

5 Transfer the pasta to a warm serving dish and pour over the sauce. Sprinkle with the Parmesan cheese, garnish with the basil, and serve immediately.

COOK'S TIP

There are many different types of clams found along almost every coast in the world. Those traditionally used in this dish are the tiny ones – only 1–2 inches across – known in Italy as vongole.

Spaghetti with Seafood Sauce

*Peeled shrimp from the freezer can become the
star ingredient in this colorful and tasty dish.*

Serves 4

INGREDIENTS

8 oz dried spaghetti, broken into 6
   inch lengths
2 tbsp olive oil
1¼ cups chicken stock
1 tsp lemon juice
1 small cauliflower, cut into florets
2 carrots, thinly sliced
4 oz snow peas
4 tbsp butter

1 onion, sliced
8 oz zucchini, sliced
1 garlic clove, minced
12 oz frozen, cooked, peeled shrimp,
   defrosted

2 tbsp chopped fresh parsley
⅓ cup freshly grated Parmesan
   cheese

½ tsp paprika
salt and pepper
4 unpeeled, cooked shrimp, to
   garnish

1 Bring a pan of lightly salted water to the boil. Add the spaghetti and 1 tbsp of the olive oil and cook until tender, but still firm to the bite. Drain the spaghetti and return to the pan. Toss with the remaining olive oil, cover, and keep warm.

2 Bring the chicken stock and lemon juice to the boil. Add the cauliflower and carrots and cook for 3–4 minutes. Remove

from the pan and set aside. Add the snow peas to the pan and cook for 1–2 minutes. Set aside with the other vegetables.

3 Melt half the butter in a skillet over a medium heat. Add the onion and zucchini and fry for about 3 minutes. Add the garlic and shrimp and cook for a further 2–3 minutes, until thoroughly heated through.

4 Stir in the reserved vegetables and heat through. Season to taste with salt and pepper and stir in the remaining butter.

5 Transfer the spaghetti to a warm serving dish. Pour over the sauce and add the chopped parsley. Toss well with 2 forks until coated. Sprinkle over the Parmesan cheese and paprika, garnish with the unpeeled shrimp, and serve immediately.

Scallops in Ginger Sauce

Scallops are both attractive and delicious and make this a special dish. Cooked with ginger and orange, this dish is perfect served with plain rice.

Serves 4

INGREDIENTS

2 tbsp vegetable oil

1 lb scallops, cleaned
and halved

1-inch piece fresh gingerroot, finely
minced

3 garlic cloves, crushed

2 leeks, shredded

$^3/_4$ cup shelled peas

$4^1/_2$ oz canned bamboo shoots,
drained and rinsed

2 tbsp light soy sauce

2 tbsp unsweetened orange juice

1 tsp superfine sugar

orange zest, to garnish

---

1 Heat the oil in a preheated wok. Add the scallops and stir-fry for 1–2 minutes. Remove the scallops from the wok with a draining spoon and set aside.

2 Add the ginger and garlic to the wok and stir-fry for 30 seconds. Stir in the leeks and peas and cook, stirring, for a further 2 minutes.

3 Add the bamboo shoots and return the scallops to the wok. Stir gently to mix without breaking up the scallops.

4 Stir in the soy sauce, orange juice, and sugar and cook for 1–2 minutes. Transfer to a serving dish, garnish with the orange zest, and serve immediately.

COOK'S TIP

The edible parts of a scallop are the round white muscle and the orange and white coral or roe. The frilly skirt surrounding the muscle – the gills and mantle – may be used for making shellfish stock. All other parts should be discarded.

COOK'S TIP

Frozen scallops may be thawed and used in this recipe, adding them at the end of cooking to prevent them from breaking up. If you are buying scallops already shelled, check whether they are fresh or frozen. Fresh scallops are cream colored and more translucent, while frozen scallops tend to be pure white.

Seafood Stir-Fry

This combination of assorted seafood and tender vegetables delicately flavored with ginger makes an ideal light meal served with thread noodles.

Serves 4

INGREDIENTS

3¹/₂ oz small, thin asparagus spears, trimmed

1 tbsp sunflower oil

1 inch piece gingerroot, cut into thin strips

1 medium leek, shredded

2 medium carrots, julienned

3¹/₂ oz baby corn-on-the-cobs, quartered lengthwise

2 tbsp light soy sauce

1 tbsp oyster sauce

1 tsp honey

1 lb cooked, assorted shellfish, thawed if frozen

freshly cooked egg noodles, to serve

TO GARNISH:

4 large cooked prawns

small bunch fresh chives

1 Bring a small saucepan of water to the boil and blanch the asparagus for 1–2 minutes. Drain the asparagus, set aside, and keep warm.

2 Heat the oil in a wok or large skillet and stir-fry the ginger, leek, carrot, and corn for about 3 minutes.

3 Add the soy sauce, oyster sauce, and honey to the wok or skillet. Stir in the shellfish and

continue to stir-fry for 2–3 minutes until the vegetables are just tender and the shellfish are thoroughly heated through. Add the blanched asparagus and stir-fry for about 2 minutes.

4 To serve, pile the cooked noodles on to 4 warm serving plates, and spoon over the seafood and vegetable stir fry. Serve garnished with a large prawn and freshly snipped chives.

COOK'S TIP

When you are preparing dense vegetables, such as carrots and other root vegetables, for stir frying, slice them into thin, evenly sized pieces so that they cook quickly and at the same rate. Delicate vegetables, such as bell peppers, leeks, and scallions, do not need to be cut as thinly.

Seared Scallops with Butter Sauce

Scallops have a terrific, subtle flavor which is complemented by this buttery sauce.

Serves 4

INGREDIENTS

1 lb scallops, without roe
6 scallions

2 tbsp vegetable oil
1 green chili, seeded and sliced

3 tbsp sweet soy sauce
1½ tbsp butter, cubed

1 Rinse the scallops under cold running water, then pat the scallops dry with absorbent paper towels.

2 Using a sharp knife, slice each scallop in half horizontally.

3 Using a sharp knife, trim and slice the scallions.

4 Heat the vegetable oil in a large preheated wok.

5 Add the chili, scallions, and scallops to the wok and stir-fry over a high heat for 4–5 minutes, or until the scallops are just cooked through.

6 Add the soy sauce and butter to the scallop stir-fry and heat through until the butter melts.

7 Transfer to warm serving bowls and serve hot.

COOK'S TIP

If you buy scallops on the shell, slide a knife underneath the membrane to loosen and cut off the tough muscle that holds the scallop to the shell. Discard the black stomach sac and intestinal vein.

COOK'S TIP

Use frozen scallops if preferred, but make sure they are completely defrosted before cooking. In addition, do not overcook them as they will easily disintegrate.

Bacon & Scallop Skewers

Wrapping bacon around the scallops helps to protect the delicate flesh from the intense heat and allows them to cook without becoming tough. The bacon also imparts a subtle smoky flavor to the scallops.

Makes 4

INGREDIENTS

grated peel and juice of $^1/_2$ lemon	12 scallops	1 yellow bell pepper
4 tbsp sunflower oil	1 red bell pepper	6 rashers smoked streaky bacon
$^1/_2$ tsp dried dill	1 green bell pepper	

1 Mix together the lemon peel and juice, oil, and dill in a nonmetallic dish. Add the scallops and mix thoroughly to coat in the marinade. Leave to marinate for 1–2 hours.

2 Cut the red, green, and yellow bell peppers in half and seed them. Cut the bell pepper halves into 1 inch pieces and then set aside until required.

3 Carefully remove the peel from the bacon. Stretch the bacon rashers with the back of a knife, then cut each bacon rasher in half.

4 Remove the scallops from the marinade, reserving any excess marinade. Wrap a piece of bacon around each scallop.

5 Thread the bacon-wrapped scallops on to skewers, alternating with the bell pepper pieces.

6 Grill the bacon and scallop skewers over hot coals for about 5 minutes, basting frequently with the lemon and oil marinade.

7 Transfer the bacon and scallop skewers to serving plates and serve at once.

VARIATION

Peel 4–8 raw shrimp and add them to the marinade with the scallops. Thread them on to the skewers alternately with the scallops and bell peppers.

COOK'S TIP

Hold the skewers with potholders when you are turning them on the grill.

Stir-Fried Squid with Green Bell Peppers & Black Bean Sauce

Squid really is wonderful if quickly cooked as in this recipe, and contrary to popular belief it is not tough and rubbery unless it is overcooked.

Serves 4

INGREDIENTS

1 lb squid rings
2 tbsp all-purpose flour
$^1/_2$ tsp salt
1 green bell pepper
2 tbsp peanut oil

1 red onion, sliced
$5^3/_4$ oz jar black bean sauce

1 Rinse the squid rings under cold running water and pat dry with paper towels.

2 Place the all-purpose flour and salt in a bowl and mix together. Add the squid rings and toss until they are finely coated.

3 Using a sharp knife, seed the bell pepper. Slice the bell pepper into thin strips.

4 Heat the peanut oil in a large preheated wok.

5 Add the bell pepper and red onion to the wok and stir-fry for about 2 minutes, or until the vegetables are just beginning to soften.

6 Add the squid rings to the wok and cook for a further 5 minutes, or until the squid is cooked through.

COOK'S TIP

Serve this recipe with fried rice or noodles tossed in soy sauce, if you wish.

Crab in Ginger Sauce

In this recipe, the crabs are served in the shell for ease and visual effect and coated in a glossy ginger sauce.

Serves 4

INGREDIENTS

2 small cooked crabs

2 tbsp vegetable oil

3-inch piece fresh
   gingerroot, grated

2 garlic cloves, thinly sliced

1 green bell pepper, seeded and cut
   into thin strips

6 scallions, cut into 1-inch lengths

2 tbsp dry sherry

$^{1}/_{2}$ tsp sesame oil

$^{2}/_{3}$ cup fish stock

1 tsp light brown sugar

2 tsp cornstarch

$^{2}/_{3}$ cup water

---

1 Rinse the crabs and gently loosen around the shell at the top. Using a sharp knife, cut away the grey tissue and discard. Rinse the crabs again.

2 Twist off the legs and claws from the crabs. Using a pair of crab claw crackers or a cleaver, gently crack the claws to break through the shell to expose the flesh. Remove and discard any loose pieces of shell.

3 Separate the body and discard the inedible lungs and sac.

Cut down the center of each crab to separate the body into two pieces and then cut each of these in half again.

4 Heat the oil in a preheated wok. Add the ginger and garlic and stir-fry for 1 minute. Add the crab pieces and stir-fry for 1 minute.

5 Stir in the bell pepper, scallions, sherry, sesame oil, stock, and sugar. Bring to the boil, reduce the heat, cover and simmer for 3–4 minutes.

6 Blend the cornstarch with the remaining water and stir it into the wok. Bring to the boil, stirring, until the sauce is thickened and clear. Transfer to a warm serving dish and serve immediately.

COOK'S TIP

If preferred, remove the crabmeat from the shells prior to stir-frying and add to the wok with the bell pepper.

Fresh-Baked Sardines

Here, fresh sardines are baked with eggs, herbs, and vegetables to form a dish similar to an omelet.

Serves 4

INGREDIENTS

2 tbsp olive oil

2 large onions, sliced into rings

3 garlic cloves, minced

2 large zucchini, cut into sticks

3 tbsp fresh thyme, stalks removed

8 sardine fillets or about 2 lb 4 oz
   whole sardines, filleted

2³/₄ oz Parmesan cheese, grated

4 eggs, beaten

²/₃ pint milk

salt and pepper

1 Heat 1 tablespoon of the oil in a skillet. Add the onions and garlic and sauté for 2–3 minutes.

2 Add the zucchini to the skillet and cook for about 5 minutes or until golden.

3 Stir 2 tablespoons of the thyme into the mixture.

4 Place half of the onions and zucchini in the base of a large ovenproof dish. Top with the sardine fillets and half of the Parmesan cheese.

5 Place the remaining onions and zucchini on top and sprinkle with the remaining thyme.

6 Mix the eggs and milk together in a bowl and season to taste with salt and pepper. Pour the mixture over the vegetables and sardines in the dish. Sprinkle the remaining Parmesan cheese over the top.

7 Bake in a preheated oven at 350°F for 20–25 minutes or until golden and set. Serve hot, straight from the oven.

VARIATION

If you cannot find sardines that are large enough to fillet, use small mackerel instead.

Fried Fish with Coconut & Basil

Fish curries are sensational and this Thai curry is no exception. Red curry and coconut are fantastic flavors with the fried fish.

Serves 4

INGREDIENTS

2 tbsp vegetable oil
1 lb skinless cod fillet
1/4 cup seasoned flour
1 clove garlic, minced

2 tbsp red Thai curry paste
1 tbsp fish sauce
1 1/4 cups coconut milk

6 oz cherry tomatoes, halved
20 fresh basil leaves
fragrant rice, to serve

1 Heat the vegetable oil in a large preheated wok.

2 Using a sharp knife, cut the fish into large cubes, taking care to remove any bones with a pair of tweezers.

3 Place the seasoned flour in a bowl. Add the cubes of fish and mix until well coated.

4 Add the coated fish to the wok and stir-fry over a high heat for 3–4 minutes, or until the fish just begins to brown at the edges.

5 Mix together the garlic, curry paste, fish sauce, and coconut milk in a bowl. Pour the mixture over the fish and bring to the boil.

6 Add the tomatoes to the mixture in the wok and leave to simmer for 5 minutes.

7 Roughly chop or tear the fresh basil leaves. Add the basil to the wok, stir carefully to combine, taking care not to break up the cubes of fish.

8 Transfer to serving plates and serve hot with fragrant rice.

COOK'S TIP

Take care not to overcook the dish once the tomatoes are added, otherwise they break down and the skins come away.

Citrus Fish Skewers

You can use your favorite fish for this dish as long as it is firm enough to thread on to a skewer. The tang of orange makes this a refreshing light meal.

Serves 4

INGREDIENTS

1 lb firm white fish fillets (such as cod or angler fish)
41 lb thick salmon fillet
2 large oranges
1 pink grapefruit

1 bunch fresh bay leaves
1 tsp finely grated lemon peel
3 tbsp lemon juice
2 tsp honey
2 garlic cloves, minced

salt and pepper

TO SERVE:
crusty bread
mixed salad

1 Skin the white fish and the salmon, rinse, and pat dry on absorbent paper towels. Cut each fillet into 16 pieces.

2 Using a sharp knife, remove the skin and pith from the oranges and grapefruit. Cut out the segments of flesh, removing all remaining traces of the pith and dividing membrane.

3 Thread the pieces of fish alternately with the orange and grapefruit segments and the bay leaves on to 8 skewers. Place the skewers in a shallow dish.

4 Mix together the lemon peel and juice, the honey, and garlic. Pour over the fish skewers and season well. Cover and chill for 2 hours, turning occasionally.

5 Preheat the broiler to medium. Remove the skewers from the marinade and place on the rack. Cook for 7–8 minutes, turning once, until cooked through.

6 Drain, transfer to serving plates, and serve with crusty bread and a fresh salad.

VARIATION

This dish makes an unusual appetizer. Try it with any firm fish – swordfish or shark, for example – or with tuna for a meatier texture.

Potato-Topped Cod

This simple dish has a spicy breadcrumb mixture topping layers of cod and potatoes. It is cooked in the oven until crisp and golden.

Serves 4

INGREDIENTS

$^1/_4$ cup butter
4 waxy potatoes, sliced
1 large onion, finely minced
1 tsp wholegrain mustard
1 tsp garam masala

pinch of chili powder
1 tbsp chopped fresh dill
$1^1/_4$ cups fresh bread crumbs

4 cod fillets, about 6 oz each
$1^3/_4$ oz Gruyère cheese, grated
salt and pepper
fresh dill sprigs, to garnish

1 Melt half of the butter in a skillet. Add the potatoes and fry for 5 minutes, turning until they are browned all over. Remove the potatoes from the pan with a draining spoon.

2 Add the remaining butter to the skillet and stir in the onion, mustard, garam masala, chili powder, chopped dill, and bread crumbs. Cook for 1-2 minutes, stirring and mixing well.

3 Layer half of the potatoes in the base of an ovenproof dish and place the cod fillets on top. Cover the cod fillets with the rest of the potato slices. Season to taste with salt and pepper.

4 Spoon the spicy mixture from the skillet over the potato and sprinkle with the grated cheese.

5 Cook in a preheated oven at 400°F for 20-25 minutes or until the topping is golden and crisp and the fish is cooked through. Garnish with fresh dill sprigs and serve at once.

VARIATION

You can use any fish for this recipe: for special occasions use salmon steaks or fillets.

COOK'S TIP

This dish is ideal served with baked vegetables, which can be cooked in the oven at the same time.

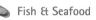

Salt Cod Fritters

These tasty little fried cakes of mashed salt cod mixed with fennel and a little chili
make an excellent snack or main course served with vegetables and a chili relish.

Makes 28 cakes

INGREDIENTS

3¹/₂ oz self-rising flour
1 egg, beaten
²/₃ cup milk
9 oz salt cod, soaked overnight

1 small red onion, finely minced
1 small fennel bulb, finely minced
1 red chili, finely minced
2 tbsp oil

TO SERVE:
crisp salad, chili relish, cooked rice,
   and fresh vegetables

1 Sift the flour into a large bowl. Make a well in the center of the flour and add the egg.

2 Using a wooden spoon, gradually draw in the flour, slowly adding the milk, and mix to form a smooth batter. Leave to stand for 10 minutes.

3 Drain the salt cod and rinse it under cold running water. Drain again thoroughly.

4 Remove and discard the skin and any bones from the fish, then mash the flesh with a fork.

5 Place the fish in a large bowl and combine with the onion, fennel, and chili. Add the mixture to the batter and blend together.

6 Heat the oil in a large skillet and, taking about 1 tablespoon of the mixture at a time, spoon it into the hot oil. Cook the fritters, in batches, for 3–4 minutes on each side until golden and slightly puffed. Keep warm while cooking the remaining mixture.

7 Serve with salad and a chili relish for a light meal or with vegetables and rice.

COOK'S TIP

If you prefer larger fritters, use
2 tablespoons per fritter and cook
for slightly longer.

Marinated Fish

Marinating fish, for even a short period, adds a subtle flavor to the flesh and makes even simply broiled or fried fish a delicious dish.

Serves 4

INGREDIENTS

4 whole mackerel, cleaned and
  gutted
4 tbsp chopped marjoram

2 tbsp extra virgin olive oil
finely grated peel and juice of 1 lime

2 garlic cloves, minced
salt and pepper

1 Under gently running water, scrape the mackerel with the blunt side of a knife to remove any scales.

2 Using a sharp knife, make a slit in the stomach of the fish and cut horizontally along until the knife will go no further very easily. Gut the fish and rinse under water. You may prefer to remove the heads before cooking, but it is not necessary.

3 Using a sharp knife, cut 4–5 diagonal slashes on each side of the fish. Place the fish in a shallow, nonmetallic dish.

4 To make the marinade, mix together the marjoram, olive oil, lime peel and juice, garlic, and salt and pepper in a bowl.

5 Pour the mixture over the fish. Leave to marinate in the refrigerator for 30 minutes.

6 Cook the mackerel, under a preheated broiler, for 5–6 minutes on each side, brushing occasionally with the reserved marinade, until golden.

7 Transfer the fish to serving plates. Pour over any remaining marinade before serving.

COOK'S TIP

If the lime is too hard to squeeze, microwave on high power for 30 seconds to release the juice. This dish is also excellent cooked on the grill.

Celery & Salt Cod Casserole

Salt cod is dried and salted in order to preserve it. It has an unusual flavor, which goes particularly well with celery in this dish.

Serves 4

INGREDIENTS

9 oz salt cod, soaked overnight
1 tbsp oil
4 shallots, finely minced
2 garlic cloves, minced

3 celery stalks, minced
1 x 14 oz can tomatoes, minced
$^2/_3$ cup fish stock

$1^3/_4$ oz pine nuts
2 tbsp roughly chopped tarragon
2 tbsp capers
crusty bread or mashed potato, to serve

1 Drain the salt cod, rinse it under plenty of running water, and drain again thoroughly. Remove and discard any skin and bones. Pat the fish dry with paper towels and cut it into chunks.

2 Heat the oil in a large skillet. Add the shallots and garlic and cook for 2–3 minutes. Add the celery, cook for a further 2 minutes, and add the tomatoes and stock.

3 Bring the mixture to the boil, reduce the heat, and leave to simmer for 5 minutes.

4 Add the fish and cook for 10 minutes or until tender.

5 Meanwhile, place the pine nuts on a cookie sheet. Place under a preheated broiler and toast for 2–3 minutes or until golden.

6 Stir the tarragon, capers, and pine nuts into the fish casserole and heat gently to warm through.

7 Transfer to serving plates and serve with fresh crusty bread or mashed potato.

COOK'S TIP

Salt cod is a useful ingredient to keep in the storecupboard and once soaked, can be used in the same way as any other fish. It does, however, have a stronger flavor than normal, and it is slightly salty. It can be found in fish stores, larger supermarkets, and delicatessens.

Stir-Fried Cod with Mango

Fish and fruit are a classic combination, and in this recipe a tropical flavor is added which gives a great scented taste to the dish.

Serves 4

INGREDIENTS

6 oz carrots	1 lb skinless cod fillet	1 tbsp lime juice
2 tbsp vegetable oil	1 ripe mango	1 tbsp chopped cilantro
1 red onion, sliced	1 tsp cornstarch	
1 red bell pepper, seeded and sliced	1 tbsp soy sauce	
1 green bell pepper, seeded and sliced	1⅓ cup tropical fruit juice	

1 Using a sharp knife, slice the carrots into thin sticks.

2 Heat the vegetable oil in a preheated wok.

3 Add the onions, carrots, and bell peppers to the wok and stir-fry for 5 minutes.

4 Using a sharp knife, cut the cod into small cubes.

5 Peel the mango, then carefully remove the flesh from the center stone. Cut the flesh into thin slices.

6 Add the cod and mango to the wok and stir-fry for a further 4–5 minutes, or until the fish is cooked through. Do not stir the mixture too much or you may break the fish up.

7 Mix the cornstarch, soy sauce, fruit juice, and lime juice in a small bowl.

8 Pour the cornstarch mixture over the stir-fry and allow the mixture to bubble and the juices to thicken. Scatter with cilantro and serve immediately.

VARIATION

You can use papaya as an alternative to the mango, if you prefer.

Steamed Fish with Black Bean Sauce

The Chinese use a lot of whole fish in their cooking, and steaming is one of their preferred methods. It helps maintain both the flavor and the texture.

Serves 4

INGREDIENTS

2 lb whole snapper, cleaned and scaled
3 garlic cloves, crushed
2 tbsp black bean sauce
1 tsp cornstarch

2 tsp sesame oil
2 tbsp light soy sauce
2 tsp superfine sugar
2 tbsp dry sherry
1 small leek, shredded

1 small red bell pepper, seeded and cut into thin strips
shredded leek and lemon wedges, to garnish
boiled rice or noodles, to serve

1 Rinse the fish inside and out with cold running water and pat dry with paper towels. Make 2-3 diagonal slashes in the flesh on each side of the fish, using a sharp knife. Rub the garlic into the fish.

2 Thoroughly mix the black bean sauce, cornstarch, sesame oil, light soy sauce, sugar, and dry sherry together in a bowl. Place the fish in a shallow heatproof dish and pour the sauce mixture over the top.

3 Sprinkle the leek and bell pepper strips on top of the sauce. Place the dish in the top of a steamer, cover, and steam for 10 minutes, or until the fish is cooked through. Transfer to a serving dish, garnish with shredded leek and lemon wedges, and serve with boiled rice or noodles.

VARIATION

Whole sea bream or sea bass may be used in this recipe instead of snapper, if you prefer.

COOK'S TIP

Insert the point of a sharp knife into the fish to test if it is cooked. The fish is cooked through if the knife goes into the flesh easily.

Herrings with Hot Pesto Sauce

*By making a simple pesto sauce, but omitting the cheese, it is possible to heat
the paste without it becoming stringy, so it can be used as a hot sauce.*

Serves 4

INGREDIENTS

4 whole herrings or small mackerel, cleaned and gutted	8 oz tomatoes, peeled, seeded and chopped	about 30 fresh basil leaves
2 tbsp olive oil	8 canned anchovy fillets, chopped	1¾ oz pine nuts
		2 garlic cloves, minced

1 Cook the herrings under a preheated broiler for about 8-10 minutes on each side, or until the skin is slightly charred on both sides.

2 Meanwhile, heat 1 tablespoon of the olive oil in a large saucepan.

3 Add the tomatoes and anchovies to the saucepan and cook over a medium heat for 5 minutes.

4 Meanwhile, place the basil, pine nuts, garlic, and remaining oil into a food processor and blend to form a smooth paste. Alternatively, pound the ingredients by hand in a mortar and pestle.

5 Add the pesto mixture to the saucepan containing the tomato and anchovy mixture and stir to heat through.

6 Spoon some of the pesto sauce on to warm individual serving plates. Place the fish on top and pour the rest of the pesto sauce over the fish. Serve immediately.

COOK'S TIP

*Try grilling the fish
for an extra char-grilled flavor,
if you prefer.*

Stir-Fried Salmon with Pineapple

Presentation plays a major part in Chinese cooking and this dish demonstrates this perfectly with the wonderful combination of colors.

Serves 4

INGREDIENTS

1 cup baby corn-n-the-cobs, halved

2 tbsp sunflower oil

1 red onion, sliced

1 orange bell pepper, seeded and
  sliced

1 green bell pepper, seeded and sliced

1 lb salmon fillet, skin removed

1 tbsp paprika

8 oz can cubed pineapple, drained

1 cup beansprouts

2 tbsp tomato catsup

2 tbsp soy sauce

2 tbsp medium sherry

1 tsp cornstarch

1 Using a sharp knife, cut the baby corns in half.

2 Heat the sunflower oil in a large preheated wok. Add the onion, bell peppers, and baby corn cobs to the wok and stir-fry for 5 minutes.

3 Rinse the salmon fillet under cold running water and pat dry with absorbent paper towels.

4 Cut the salmon flesh into thin strips and place in a large bowl. Sprinkle with the paprika and toss until well coated.

5 Add the salmon to the wok together with the pineapple and stir-fry for a further 2–3 minutes or until the fish is tender.

6 Add the beansprouts to the wok and toss well.

7 Mix together the tomato catsup, soy sauce, sherry and cornstarch. Add the mixture to the wok and cook until the juices start to thicken. Transfer to warm serving plates and serve immediately.

VARIATION

You can use trout fillets instead of the salmon as an alternative, if you prefer.

Five-Spice Salmon with Ginger Stir-Fry

Five-spice powder is a blend of star anise, fennel, cinnamon, cloves, and Szechuan peppercorns that is often used in Chinese dishes. It is a deliciously fragrant seasoning.

Serves 4

INGREDIENTS

4 salmon fillets, skinned, 4 oz each
2 tsp five-spice powder
pepper
1 large leek
1 large carrot
4 oz snow peas

1 inch piece gingerroot
2 tbsp ginger wine
2 tbsp light soy sauce
1 tbsp vegetable oil
freshly boiled noodles, to serve

TO GARNISH:
leek, shredded
gingerroot, shredded
carrot, shredded

1 Wash the salmon and pat dry on absorbent paper towels. Rub the five-spice powder into both sides of the fish and season with freshly ground pepper. Set aside until required.

2 Trim the leek, slice it down the center, and rinse under cold water to remove any dirt. Finely shred the leek. Peel the carrot and cut it into very thin strips. Top and tail the snow peas and cut them into shreds. Peel the ginger and slice thinly into strips.

3 Place all of the vegetables into a large bowl and toss in the ginger wine and 1 tbsp soy sauce. Set aside.

4 Preheat the broiler to medium. Place the salmon fillets on the rack and brush with the remaining soy sauce. Cook for 2–3 minutes on each side until cooked through.

5 While the salmon is cooking, heat the oil in a non-stick wok or large skillet and stir-fry the vegetables for 5 minutes until just tender. Take care that you do not overcook the vegetables – they should still have bite. Transfer to serving plates.

6 Drain the salmon on kitchen paper and serve on a bed of stir-fried vegetables. Garnish with shredded leek, ginger, and carrot and serve with noodles.

Teriyaki Stir-Fried Salmon with Crispy Leeks

Teriyaki is a wonderful Japanese dish which is delicious when made with salmon and served on a bed of crispy leeks.

Serves 4

INGREDIENTS

1 lb salmon fillet, skinned	1 tsp rice wine vinegar	4 tbsp corn oil
2 tbsp sweet soy sauce	1 tbsp demerara sugar	1 lb leeks, thinly shredded
2 tbsp tomato catsup	1 clove garlic, crushed	finely minced red chilies, to garnish

1 Using a sharp knife, cut the salmon into slices. Place the slices of salmon in a shallow nonmetallic dish.

2 Mix together the soy sauce, tomato catsup, rice wine vinegar, sugar, and garlic.

3 Pour the mixture over the salmon, toss well, and leave to marinate for about 30 minutes.

4 Meanwhile, heat 3 tablespoons of the corn oil in a large preheated wok.

5 Add the leeks to the wok and stir-fry over a medium high heat for about 10 minutes, or until the leeks become crispy and tender.

6 Using a draining spoon, carefully remove the leeks from the wok and transfer to warmed serving plates.

7 Add the remaining oil to the wok. Add the salmon and the marinade to the wok and cook for 2 minutes. Spoon over the leeks, garnish, and serve immediately.

VARIATION

You can use a tenderloin of beef instead of the salmon, if you prefer.

Spaghetti with Smoked Salmon

*Made in moments, this is a luxurious dish
to astonish and delight unexpected guests.*

Serves 4

INGREDIENTS

1 lb dried buckwheat spaghetti

2 tbsp olive oil

$\frac{1}{2}$ cup crumbled
  feta cheese

salt

fresh cilantro or parsley leaves, to
  garnish

SAUCE:

$1\frac{1}{4}$ cups heavy cream

$\frac{5}{8}$ cup whiskey or brandy

$4\frac{1}{2}$ oz smoked salmon

pinch of cayenne pepper

black pepper

2 tbsp chopped fresh cilantro or
  parsley

---

1 Bring a large pan of lightly salted water to the boil. Add the spaghetti and 1 tbsp of the olive oil and cook until tender, but still firm to the bite. Drain the spaghetti, return to the pan, and sprinkle over the remaining olive oil. Cover, shake the pan, set aside, and keep warm.

2 Pour the cream into a small saucepan and bring to simmering point, but do not let it boil. Pour the whiskey or brandy into another small saucepan and bring to simmering point, but do not allow it to boil. Remove both pans from the heat and mix together the cream and whiskey or brandy.

3 Cut the smoked salmon into thin strips and add to the cream mixture. Season to taste with cayenne and black pepper. Just before serving, stir in the chopped fresh cilantro or parsley.

4 Transfer the spaghetti to a warm serving dish, pour over the sauce, and toss thoroughly with 2 large forks. Scatter over the crumbled feta cheese, garnish with the cilantro or parsley leaves, and serve immediately.

COOK'S TIP

*Serve this rich and luxurious dish
with a green salad tossed in a
lemony dressing.*

Poached Salmon Steaks with Penne

Fresh salmon and pasta in a mouth-watering lemon and
watercress sauce – a wonderful summer evening treat.

Serves 4

INGREDIENTS

4 x 10 oz fresh salmon steaks

4 tbsp butter

$3/4$ cup dry white wine

sea salt

8 peppercorns

fresh dill sprig

fresh tarragon sprig

1 lemon, sliced

1 lb dried penne

2 tbsp olive oil

lemon slices and fresh watercress,
  to garnish

LEMON & WATERCRESS SAUCE:

2 tbsp butter

$1/4$ cup all purpose flour

$5/8$ cup warm milk

juice and finely grated peel of
  2 lemons

2 oz watercress, chopped

salt and pepper

1 Put the salmon in a large, non-stick pan. Add the butter, wine, a pinch of sea salt, the peppercorns, dill, tarragon, and lemon. Cover, bring to the boil, and simmer for 10 minutes.

2 Using a fish slice, carefully remove the salmon. Strain and reserve the cooking liquid. Remove and discard the salmon skin and center bones. Place on a warm dish, cover, and keep warm.

3 Meanwhile, bring a saucepan of salted water to the boil. Add the penne and 1 tbsp of the oil and cook for 12 minutes until tender but still firm to the bite. Drain and sprinkle over the remaining olive oil. Place on a warm serving dish, top with the salmon steaks, and keep warm.

4 To make the sauce, melt the butter and stir in the flour for 2 minutes. Stir in the milk and

about 7 tbsp of the reserved cooking liquid. Add the lemon juice and peel and cook, stirring, for a further 10 minutes.

5 Add the watercress to the sauce, stir gently, and season to taste with salt and pepper.

6 Pour the sauce over the salmon and penne, garnish with slices of lemon and fresh watercress, and serve immediately.

Sole Fillets in Marsala & Cream

A rich wine and cream sauce makes this an excellent dinner party dish. You can make the stock the day before so it takes only minutes to cook and serve the fish.

Serves 4

INGREDIENTS

STOCK:
2^1/$_2$ cups water
bones and skin from the sole fillets
1 onion, peeled and halved
1 carrot, peeled and halved
3 fresh bay leaves

SAUCE;
1 tbsp olive oil
1 tbsp butter
4 shallots, finely minced
3^1/$_2$ oz baby button mushrooms,
   wiped and halved

1 tbsp peppercorns, lightly crushed
8 sole fillets
^{1}/$_3$ cup Marsala
^{2}/$_3$ pint heavy cream

1 To make the stock, place the water, fish bones and skin, onion, carrot, and bay leaves in a saucepan and bring to the boil.

2 Reduce the heat and leave the mixture to simmer for 1 hour or until the stock has reduced to about ^{2}/$_3$ cup. Drain the stock through a fine sifter, discarding the bones and vegetables, and set aside.

3 To make the sauce, heat the oil and butter in a skillet. Add the shallots, and cook, stirring, for 2–3 minutes or until just softened.

4 Add the mushrooms to the skillet and cook, stirring, for a further 2–3 minutes or until they are just beginning to brown.

5 Add the peppercorns and sole fillets to the skillet. Fry the sole fillets for 3–4 minutes on each side or until golden brown.

6 Pour the wine and stock over the fish and leave to simmer for 3 minutes. Remove the fish with a fish slice or a draining spoon, set aside, and keep warm.

7 Increase the heat and boil the mixture in the pan for about 5 minutes or until the sauce has reduced and thickened.

8 Pour in the cream, return the fish to the pan, and heat through. Serve with the cooked vegetables of your choice.

Fig 8 Seafood

Stir-Fried Gingered Angler Fish

This dish is a real treat and is perfect for special occasions. Angler fish has a tender flavor which is ideal with asparagus, chili, and ginger.

Serves 4

INGREDIENTS

1 lb angler fish
1 tbsp freshly grated gingerroot
2 tbsp sweet chili sauce
1 tbsp corn oil

1 cup fine asparagus
3 scallions, sliced
1 tsp sesame oil

1 Using a sharp knife, slice the angler fish into thin flat rounds.

2 Mix the ginger with the chili sauce in a small bowl.

3 Brush the ginger and chili sauce mixture over the angler fish pieces.

4 Heat the corn oil in a large preheated wok.

5 Add the angler fish, asparagus, and scallions to the wok and stir-fry for about 5 minutes.

6 Remove the wok from the heat, drizzle the sesame oil over the stir-fry, and toss well to combine.

7 Transfer to warm serving plates and serve immediately.

COOK'S TIP

Some recipes specify to grate ginger before it is cooked with other ingredients. To do this, just peel the flesh and rub it at a 45° angle up and down on the fine section of a metal grater, or use a special wooden or ceramic ginger grater.

VARIATION

Angler fish is quite expensive, but it is well worth using it as it has a wonderful flavor and texture. At a push you could use cubes of chunky cod fillet instead.

Sea Bass with Olive Sauce on a Bed of Macaroni

A favorite fish for chefs, the delicious sea bass is now becoming increasingly common in supermarkets and fish stores for family meals.

Serves 4

INGREDIENTS

1 lb dried macaroni
1 tbsp olive oil
8 x 4 oz sea bass medallions

TO GARNISH:
lemon slices
shredded leek
shredded carrot

SAUCE:
2 tbsp butter
4 shallots, minced
2 tbsp capers
1¹/₂ cups pitted green olives, minced
4 tbsp balsamic vinegar
1¹/₄ cups fish stock
1¹/₄ cups heavy cream

juice of 1 lemon
salt and pepper

1 To make the sauce, melt the butter in a skillet. Add the shallots and cook over a low heat for 4 minutes. Add the capers and olives and cook for a further 3 minutes.

2 Stir in the balsamic vinegar and fish stock, bring to the boil and reduce by half. Add the cream, stirring, and reduce again by half. Season to taste with salt

and pepper and stir in the lemon juice. Remove the pan from the heat, set aside and keep warm.

3 Bring a large saucepan of lightly salted water to the boil. Add the pasta and olive oil and cook for about 12 minutes, until tender but still firm to the bite.

4 Meanwhile, lightly broil the sea bass medallions for 3–4

minutes on each side, until cooked through but still moist and delicate.

5 Drain the pasta and transfer to large individual serving dishes. Top the pasta with the fish medallions and pour the olive sauce over. Garnish with lemon slices, shredded leek, and shredded carrot and serve immediately.

Casserole of Fusilli & Smoked Haddock with Egg Sauce

This quick, easy, and inexpensive dish would be ideal for a mid-week family supper.

Serves 4

INGREDIENTS

2 tbsp butter, plus extra for oiling

1 lb smoked haddock fillets, cut into 4 slices

2¹/₂ cups milk

¹/₄ cup all-purpose flour

pinch of freshly grated nutmeg

3 tbsp heavy cream

1 tbsp chopped fresh parsley

2 eggs, hard cooked and mashed to a pulp

4 cups dried fusilli

1 tbsp lemon juice

salt and pepper

boiled new potatoes and beet

1 Thoroughly oil a casserole with butter. Put the haddock in the casserole and pour over the milk. Bake in a preheated oven at 400°F for about 15 minutes. Carefully pour the cooking liquid into a pitcher without breaking up the fish.

2 Melt the butter in a saucepan and stir in the flour. Whisk in the reserved cooking liquid. Season to taste with salt, pepper, and nutmeg. Stir in the cream, parsley, and mashed egg and cook, stirring constantly, for 2 minutes.

3 Meanwhile, bring a large saucepan of lightly salted water to the boil. Add the fusilli and lemon juice and cook until tender, but still firm to the bite.

4 Drain the pasta and spoon or tip it over the fish. Top with the sauce and return the casserole to the oven for 10 minutes.

5 Serve the casserole with boiled new potatoes and beet.

VARIATION

You can use any type of dried pasta for this casserole. Try penne, conchiglie, or rigatoni.

Mullet with Ginger

Ginger is widely used in Chinese cooking for its strong, pungent flavour. Always use fresh ginger wherever possible, but ground can be used as an alternative.

Serves 4

INGREDIENTS

1 whole mullet, cleaned and scaled

2 spring onions, chopped

1 tsp grated fresh root ginger

120 ml/4 fl oz/$\frac{1}{2}$ cup garlic
   wine vinegar

120 ml/4 fl oz/$\frac{1}{2}$ cup light soy sauce

3 tsp caster sugar

dash of chilli sauce

120 ml/4 fl oz/$\frac{1}{2}$ cup fish stock

1 green pepper, thinly sliced

1 large tomato, skinned, seeded and
   cut into thin strips

salt and pepper

sliced tomato, to garnish

1 Rinse the fish inside and out and pat dry with paper towels.

2 Make 3 diagonal slits in the flesh on each side of the fish. Season with salt and pepper inside and out.

3 Place the fish on a heatproof plate and scatter the spring onions and ginger over the top. Cover and steam for 10 minutes, or until the fish is cooked well through.

4 Place the vinegar, soy sauce, sugar, chilli sauce, fish stock, pepper and tomato in a saucepan and bring to the boil, stirring occasionally. Cook over a high heat until the sauce has reduced slightly and thickened.

5 Remove the fish from the steamer and transfer to a warm serving dish. Pour the sauce over the fish, garnish with tomato slices and serve at once.

COOK'S TIP

Make sure that you cook the sauce for long enough so that it reduces and thickens slightly. It should not be too runny.

VARIATION

Use fillets of fish for this recipe if preferred, and reduce the cooking time to 5–7 minutes.

Vermicelli with Fillets of Red Mullet

*This simple recipe perfectly complements
the sweet flavor and delicate texture of the fish.*

Serves 4

INGREDIENTS

2¼ lb red mullet fillets
1¼ cups dry white wine
4 shallots, finely minced
1 garlic clove, minced
3 tbsp finely chopped mixed
   fresh herbs

finely grated peel and juice of
  1 lemon
pinch of freshly grated nutmeg
3 anchovy fillets, roughly chopped
2 tbsp heavy cream
1 tsp cornstarch
1 lb dried vermicelli

1 tbsp olive oil
salt and pepper

TO GARNISH:
1 fresh mint sprig
lemon slices
lemon peel

1 Put the red mullet fillets in a large casserole. Pour over the wine and add the shallots, garlic, chopped herbs, lemon peel and juice, nutmeg, and anchovies. Season to taste with salt and pepper. Cover and bake in a preheated oven at 350°F for 35 minutes.

2 Carefully transfer the mullet to a warm dish. Set aside and keep warm while you prepare the sauce and pasta.

3 Pour the cooking liquid into a pan and bring to the boil. Simmer for 25 minutes or until reduced by half. Mix together the cream and cornstarch and stir into the sauce to thicken.

4 Meanwhile, bring a large pan of lightly salted water to the boil. Add the vermicelli and olive oil and cook for 8–10 minutes, until tender, but still firm to the bite. Drain the pasta and transfer to a warm serving dish.

5 Arrange the red mullet fillets on top of the vermicelli and pour over the sauce. Garnish with a fresh mint sprig, slices of lemon and strips of lemon peel, and serve immediately.

COOK'S TIP

The best red mullet is sometimes called golden mullet, although it is bright red in color.

Spaghetti al Tonno

The classic Italian combination of pasta and tuna is enhanced in this recipe with a delicious parsley sauce.

Serves 4

INGREDIENTS

7 oz can tuna, drained
2 oz can anchovies, drained
1$\frac{1}{8}$ cups olive oil

1 cup roughly chopped flat leaf
  parsley
$\frac{5}{8}$ cup crème fraîche
1 lb dried spaghetti

2 tbsp butter
salt and pepper
black olives, to garnish
crusty bread, to serve

1 Remove any bones from the tuna. Put the tuna into a food processor or blender, together with the anchovies, 1 cup of the olive oil, and the flat leaf parsley. Process until the sauce is smooth.

2 Spoon the crème fraîche into the food processor or blender and process again for a few seconds to blend thoroughly. Season to taste with salt and black pepper.

3 Bring a large pan of lightly salted water to the boil. Add the spaghetti and the remaining olive oil and cook until tender, but still firm to the bite.

4 Drain the spaghetti, return to the pan, and place over a medium heat. Add the butter and toss well to coat. Spoon in the sauce and quickly toss into the spaghetti, using 2 forks.

5 Remove the pan from the heat and divide the spaghetti between 4 warm individual serving plates. Garnish with the olives and serve immediately with warm, crusty bread.

VARIATION

If liked, you can add 1–2 garlic cloves to the sauce, substitute ½ cup chopped fresh basil for half the parsley, and garnish with capers instead of black olives.

Tuna Steaks with Fragrant Spices & Lime

Fresh tuna steaks are very meaty – they have a firm texture, yet the flesh is succulent. This recipe would be an impressive addition to a barbecue.

Serves 4

INGREDIENTS

4 tuna steaks, 6 oz each
1/2 tsp finely grated lime peel
1 garlic clove, minced
2 tsp olive oil
1 tsp ground cumin

1 tsp ground coriander
pepper
1 tbsp lime juice
2 tbsp chopped fresh cilantro

TO SERVE:
avocado relish (see Cook's Tip, below)
lime wedges

1 Trim the skin from the tuna steaks, rinse, and pat dry on absorbent paper towels.

2 In a small bowl, mix together the lime peel, garlic, olive oil, cumin, coriander, and pepper to make a paste.

3 Spread the paste thinly on both sides of the tuna. Heat a non-stick, ridged skillet until hot and press the tuna steaks into the pan to seal them. Lower the heat and cook for 5 minutes. Turn the fish over and cook for a further 4–5 minutes until the fish is cooked through. Drain on absorbent paper towels and transfer to a serving plate.

4 Sprinkle the lime juice and chopped cilantro over the fish. Serve with freshly made avocado relish (see Cook's Tip, right) and lime wedges.

COOK'S TIP

For low-fat avocado relish to serve with tuna, peel and remove the stone from one small ripe avocado. Toss in 1 tbsp lime juice. Mix in 1 tbsp freshly chopped cilantro and 1 small finely minced red onion. Stir in some chopped fresh mango or a minced medium tomato and season well.

Trout with Pineapple

Pineapple is widely used in Chinese cooking. The tartness of fresh pineapple complements fish particularly well.

Serves 4

INGREDIENTS

4 trout fillets, skinned
2 tbsp vegetable oil
2 garlic cloves, cut into slivers
4 slices fresh pineapple, peeled
   and diced

1 celery stalk, sliced
1 tbsp light soy sauce
$^1/_4$ cup fresh or unsweetened
   pineapple juice
$^2/_3$ cup fish stock

1 tsp cornstarch
2 tsp water
shredded celery leaves and fresh red
   chili strips, to garnish

1 Cut the trout fillets into strips. Heat 1 tablespoon of the vegetable oil in a preheated wok until almost smoking. Reduce the heat slightly, add the fish, and sauté for 2 minutes. Remove from the wok and set aside.

2 Add the remaining oil to the wok, reduce the heat, and add the garlic, pineapple, and celery. Stir-fry for 1–2 minutes.

3 Add the soy sauce, pineapple juice, and fish stock to the wok. Bring to the boil and cook, stirring, for 2–3 minutes, or until the sauce has reduced.

4 Blend the cornstarch with the water to form a paste and stir it into the wok. Bring the sauce to the boil and cook, stirring constantly, until the sauce thickens and clears.

5 Return the fish to the wok, and cook, stirring gently, until heated through. Transfer to a warmed serving dish and serve, garnished with shredded celery leaves and red chili strips.

COOK'S TIP

Use canned pineapple instead of fresh pineapple if you wish, choosing slices in unsweetened, natural juice in preference to a syrup.

Genoese Seafood Risotto

The Genoese risotto is cooked in a different way from any of the other risottos. First, you cook the rice, then you prepare a sauce, then you mix the two together. The results are just as delicious though!

Serves 4

INGREDIENTS

5 cups hot fish or chicken stock
12 oz risotto rice, washed
3 tbsp butter

2 garlic cloves, minced
9 oz mixed seafood, preferably raw, such as shrimp, squid, mussels, clams, and shrimps

2 tbsp chopped oregano, plus extra for garnishing
$1^3/_4$ oz pecorino or Parmesan cheese, grated

1 In a large saucepan, bring the stock to the boil. Add the rice and cook for about 12 minutes, stirring, until the rice is tender or according to the instructions on the packet. Drain thoroughly, reserving any excess liquid.

2 Heat the butter in a large skillet and add the garlic, stirring.

3 Add the raw mixed seafood to the skillet and cook for 5 minutes. If the seafood is already cooked, fry for 2–3 minutes.

4 Stir the oregano into the seafood mixture in the skillet.

5 Add the cooked rice to the pan and cook for 2–3 minutes, stirring, or until hot. Add the reserved stock if the mixture gets too sticky.

6 Add the pecorino or Parmesan cheese and mix well.

7 Transfer the risotto to warm serving dishes and serve immediately.

COOK'S TIP

The Genoese are excellent cooks, and they make particularly delicious fish dishes flavored with the local olive oil.

Sweet & Sour Fish Salad

This refreshing blend of pink and white fishes mixed with fresh pineapple and bell peppers make an interesting appetizers or a light meal.

Serves 4

INGREDIENTS

8 oz trout fillets
8 oz white fish fillets (such as haddock or cod)
1¼ cups water
1 stalk lemongrass
2 lime leaves
1 large red chili
1 bunch scallions, trimmed and shredded

4 oz fresh pineapple flesh, diced
1 small red bell pepper, seeded and diced
1 bunch watercress, washed and trimmed
fresh snipped chives, to garnish

DRESSING:
1 tbsp sunflower oil
1 tbsp rice wine vinegar
pinch of chili powder
1 tsp honey
salt and pepper

1 Rinse the fish, place in a skillet, and pour over the water. Bend the lemongrass in half to bruise it and add to the pan with the lime leaves. Prick the chili with a fork and add to the pan. Bring to the boil and simmer for 7–8 minutes. Let cool.

2 Drain the fish fillet, flake the flesh away from the skin, and place in a bowl. Gently stir in the scallions, pineapple, and bell pepper.

3 Arrange the washed watercress on 4 serving plates, pile the cooked fish mixture on top, and set aside.

4 To make the dressing, mix all the ingredients together and season well. Spoon over the fish and serve garnished with chives.

VARIATION

This recipe also works very well if you replace the fish with 12 oz white crab meat. Add a dash of Tabasco sauce if you like it hot!

Baking & Desserts

The ideal ending to a meal is fresh fruit,
topped with low-fat yogurt or fromage blanc. Fruit
contains no fat and is sweet enough to need extra sugar,
but it is a valuable source of vitamins and fiber – ideal
in every way for anyone who cares about their
own and their family's health.

There are, however, dozens of other ways
in which fruit can be used as the basis for desserts
and bakes, and thanks to modern transportation
systems the range of unusual and exotic fruits available
in supermarkets seems to expand every week.
Experiment with some of these unfamiliar fruits in
delicious warm desserts, sophisticated mousses
and fools, and satisfying cakes, and use old
favorites in enticing new ways.

Baked Bananas

The orange-flavored cream can be prepared in advance but do not make up the banana packets until just before you need to grill them – they take only a few moments to get ready.

Serves 4

INGREDIENTS

4 bananas
2 passion fruit
4 tbsp orange juice
4 tbsp orange-flavored liqueur

ORANGE-FLAVORED CREAM:
$^2/_3$ cup heavy cream
3 tbsp confectioners' sugar

2 tbsp orange-flavored liqueur

1 Peel the bananas and place each one on to a sheet of kitchen foil.

2 Cut the passion fruit in half and squeeze the juice of each half over each banana. Spoon over the orange juice and liqueur.

3 Fold the kitchen foil over the top of the bananas to enclose the bananas completely.

4 Grill the bananas over hot coals for about 10 minutes or until the bananas are just tender.

5 To make the orange-flavored cream, pour the heavy cream into a mixing bowl and sprinkle over the confectioners' sugar. Whisk the mixture until it is standing in soft peaks. Carefully fold in the orange-flavored liqueur and leave to chill in the refrigerator until required.

6 Transfer the foil parcels to warm, individual serving plates. Open out the foil packers at the table and then serve with the orange-flavored cream.

VARIATION

Leave the bananas in their skins for a really quick dessert. Split the banana skins and pop in 1–2 cubes of chocolate. Wrap the bananas in kitchen foil and grill for 10 minutes, or until the chocolate just melts.

Toffee Fruit Kabobs

Serve these fruit kabobs with a sticky toffee sauce. They are perfect for fall barbecues such as Hallowe'en.

Serves 4

INGREDIENTS

2 eating apples, cored and cut into wedges

2 firm pears, cored and cut into wedges

juice of $^1/_2$ lemon

1 oz light muscovado sugar

$^1/_4$ tsp ground allspice

1 oz unsalted butter, melted

SAUCE:

$4^1/_2$ oz butter

$3^1/_2$ oz light muscovado sugar

6 tbsp heavy cream

1 Toss the apple and pears in the lemon juice to prevent any discoloration.

2 Mix the sugar and allspice together and sprinkle over the fruit.

3 Thread the fruit pieces on to skewers.

4 To make the toffee sauce, place the butter and sugar in a saucepan and heat, stirring gently, until the butter has melted and the sugar has dissolved.

5 Add the cream to the saucepan and bring to the boil. Boil for 1–2 minutes, then set aside to cool slightly.

6 Meanwhile, place the fruit kabobs over hot coals and grill for about 5 minutes, turning and basting frequently with the melted butter, until the fruit is just tender.

7 Transfer the fruit kabobs to warm serving plates and serve with the slightly cooled toffee sauce.

COOK'S TIP

Firm apples that will keep their shape are needed for this dish. Soft apples and pears will become mushy as they cook.

VARIATION

Sprinkle the fruit kabobs with chopped walnuts or pecan nuts before serving, if you wish.

Baked Apples with Blackberries

*This winter dessert is a classic dish. Large, fluffy apples are hollowed out
and filled with spices, almonds, and blackberries. Serve hot with low-fat custard.*

Serves 4

INGREDIENTS

4 medium-sized cooking apples
1 tbsp lemon juice
3^1/2 oz prepared blackberries, thawed
   if frozen
^{1}/2 oz slivered almonds

^{1}/2 tsp ground allspice
^{1}/2 tsp finely grated lemon peel
2 tbsp brown crystal sugar
1^1/4 cups ruby port
1 cinnamon stick, broken

2 tsp cornstarch blended with 2 tbsp
   cold water
low-fat custard, to serve

1 Preheat the oven to 400°F. Wash and dry the apples. Using a small sharp knife, make a shallow cut through the skin around the middle of each apple – this will help the apples to cook through.

2 Core the apples, brush the centers with the lemon juice to prevent browning, and stand in a shallow ovenproof dish.

3 In a bowl, mix together the blackberries, almonds, allspice, lemon peel, and sugar. Using a teaspoon, spoon the mixture into the center of each apple.

4 Pour the port into the tin, add the cinnamon stick, and bake the apples in the oven for 35–40 minutes or until tender and soft. Drain the cooking juices into a pan and keep the apples warm.

5 Discard the cinnamon and add the cornstarch mixture to the cooking juices. Heat, stirring, until thickened.

6 Heat the custard until very hot. Pour the sauce over the apples and serve with the custard.

VARIATION

*Use raspberries
instead of blackberries and, if you
prefer, replace the port with
unsweetened orange juice.*

Baked Pears with Cinnamon & Brown Sugar

This simple recipe is easy to prepare and cook but is deliciously warming. Serve hot with low-fat custard, or allow to cool and serve chilled with fromage blanc or yogurt.

Serves 4

INGREDIENTS

4 ripe pears

2 tbsp lemon juice

4 tbsp light muscovado sugar

1 tsp ground cinnamon

2 oz low-fat spread

low-fat custard, to serve

lemon peel, finely grated, to decorate

1 Preheat the oven to 400°F. Core and peel the pears, then slice them in half lengthwise and brush all over with the lemon juice to prevent the pears from discoloring. Place the pears, cored side down, in a small non-stick roasting pan.

2 Place the sugar, cinnamon, and low-fat spread in a small saucepan and heat gently, stirring, until the sugar has melted. Keep the heat low to stop too much water evaporating from the low-fat spread as it gets hot. Spoon the mixture over the pears.

3 Bake for 20–25 minutes or until the pears are tender and golden, occasionally spooning the sugar mixture over the fruit during the cooking time.

4 To serve, heat the custard until it is very hot and spoon over the bases of 4 warm dessert plates. Arrange 2 pear halves on each plate. Decorate with grated lemon peel and serve.

VARIATION

This recipe also works well if you use cooking apples. For alternative flavors, replace the cinnamon with ground ginger and serve the pears sprinkled with chopped stem ginger in syrup. Alternatively, use ground allspice and spoon over some warmed dark rum to serve.

Pan-Cooked Apples in Red Wine

This simple combination of apples and raspberries cooked
in red wine is a colorful and tempting dessert.

Serves 4

INGREDIENTS

4 dessert apples
2 tbsp lemon juice
1$^{1}/_{2}$ oz low-fat spread
2 oz light muscovado sugar

1 small orange
1 cinnamon stick, broken
$^{2}/_{3}$ cup red wine
8 oz raspberries, hulled and thawed if frozen

sprigs of fresh mint, to decorate

1 Peel and core the apples, then cut them into thick wedges. Place the apples in a bowl and toss in the lemon juice to prevent the fruit from discoloring.

2 In a skillet, gently melt the low-fat spread over a low heat, add the sugar, and stir to form a paste.

3 Stir the apple wedges into the pan and cook, stirring, for 2 minutes until well coated in the sugar paste.

4 Using a vegetable peeler, pare off a few strips of orange peel. Add the orange peel to the pan along with the cinnamon pieces. Extract the juice from the orange and pour into the pan with the red wine. Bring to the boil, then simmer for 10 minutes, stirring.

5 Add the raspberries to the pan and cook for 5 minutes until the apples are tender.

6 Discard the orange peel and cinnamon pieces. Transfer the apple and raspberry mixture to a serving plate together with the wine sauce. Decorate with a sprig of fresh mint and serve hot.

VARIATION

For other fruity combinations, cook the apples with blackberries, blackcurrants, or redcurrants. You may need to add more sugar if you use currants as they are not as sweet as raspberries.

Fruit & Fiber Layers

A good, hearty dessert, guaranteed to fill you up.
Use your own favorite dried fruits in the compote.

Serves 4

INGREDIENTS

4 oz no-need-to-soak
   dried apricots
4 oz no-need-to-soak
   dried prunes
4 oz no-need-to-soak
   dried peaches

2 oz dried apple
1 oz dried cherries
2 cups unsweetened apple juice
6 cardamom pods
6 cloves
1 cinnamon stick, broken

$1^1/_4$ cups low-fat natural yogurt
4 oz crunchy oat cereal
apricot slices, to decorate

1 To make the fruit compote, place the dried apricots, prunes, peaches, apples, and cherries in a saucepan and pour in the apple juice.

2 Add the cardamom pods, cloves, and cinnamon stick to the pan, bring to the boil and simmer for 10–15 minutes until the fruits are plump and tender.

3 Allow the mixture to cool completely in the pan,

transfer the mixture to a bowl, and leave to chill in the refrigerator for 1 hour. Remove and discard the spices from the fruits.

4 Spoon the compote into 4 dessert glasses, layering it alternately with yogurt and oat cereal, finishing with the oat cereal on top.

5 Decorate each dessert with slices of apricot and serve at once.

COOK'S TIP

There are many dried fruits available, including mangoes and pears, some of which need soaking, so read the instructions on the packet before use. Also, check the ingredients label, because several types of dried fruit have added sugar or are rolled in sugar, and this will affect the sweetness of the dish you use them in.

Brown Sugar Pavlovas

This simple combination of fudgey meringue topped with yogurt and raspberries is the perfect finale to any meal.

Serves 4

CALORIES PER SERVING: 170 • FAT CONTENT PER SERVING: 0.2 G

INGREDIENTS

2 large egg whites	³/₄ cup low-fat unsweetened yogurt	rose-scented geranium leaves,
1 tsp cornstarch	6 oz raspberries, thawed	to decorate
1 tsp raspberry vinegar	if frozen	
3¹/₂ oz light muscovado sugar,	2 tbsp redcurrant jelly	
crushed free of lumps	2 tbsp unsweetened orange juice	

1 Preheat the oven to 300°F. Line a large baking sheet with baking parchment. In a large, grease-free bowl, whisk the egg whites until very stiff and dry. Fold in the cornstarch and vinegar.

2 Gradually whisk in the sugar, a spoonful at a time, until the mixture is thick and glossy.

3 Divide the mixture into 4 and spoon on to the baking sheet, spaced well apart. Smooth each into a round, about 4 inch across,

and bake in the oven for 40–45 minutes until browned and crisp. Leave to cool on the baking tray.

4 Place the redcurrant jelly and orange juice in a small pan and heat, stirring, until melted. Leave to cool for 10 minutes.

5 Meanwhile, using a palette knife, carefully remove each pavlova from the baking parchment and transfer to a serving plate. Top with unsweetened yogurt and raspberries.

6 Spoon over the redcurrant jelly mixture to glaze. Decorate and serve.

VARIATION

Make a large pavlova by forming the meringue into a circle, measuring 7 inches across, on a lined baking sheet and bake for 1 hour.

Grilled Fruit Platter with Lime 'Butter'

This delicious variation of a hot fruit salad includes wedges of tropical fruits, dusted with dark brown, treacly sugar, and a pinch of spice before grilling.

Serves 4

INGREDIENTS

1 baby pineapple	4 tbsp dark rum	LIME BUTTER:
1 ripe papaya	1 tsp ground allspice	2 oz low-fat spread
1 ripe mango	2 tbsp lime juice	$^{1}/_{2}$ tsp finely grated lime peel
2 kiwi fruit	4 tbsp dark muscovado sugar	1 tbsp confectioners' sugar
4 finger bananas		

1 Quarter the pineapple, trimming away most of the leaves, and place in a shallow dish. Peel the papaya, cut it in half, and scoop out the seeds. Cut the flesh into thick wedges and place in the same dish as the pineapple.

2 Peel the mango, cut either side of the smooth, central flat stone, and remove the stone. Slice the flesh into thick wedges. Peel the kiwi fruit and cut in half. Peel the bananas. Add all of these fruits to the dish.

3 Sprinkle over the rum, allspice and lime juice, cover, and leave at room temperature for 30 minutes, turning occasionally, to allow the flavors to develop.

4 Meanwhile, make the butter. Place the low-fat spread in a small bowl and beat in the lime peel and sugar until well mixed. Leave to chill until required.

5 Preheat the broiler to hot. Drain the fruit, reserving the juices, and arrange in the broiler pan. Sprinkle with the sugar and broil for 3–4 minutes until hot, bubbling, and beginning to char.

6 Transfer the fruit to a serving plate and spoon over the juices. Serve with the lime butter.

VARIATION

Serve with a light sauce of 1¹/4 cups tropical fruit juice thickened with 2 tsp arrowroot.

Rich Chocolate Loaf

*Another rich chocolate dessert, this loaf is very simple to make
and can be served as a tea-time treat as well.*

Makes 16 slices

INGREDIENTS

5$^1/_2$ oz dark chocolate

6 tbsp butter, unsalted

7$^1/_4$ oz tin sweetened condensed milk

2 tsp cinnamon

2$^3/_4$ oz almonds

2$^3/_4$ oz amaretti cookies, broken

1$^3/_4$ oz dried no-need-to-soak
apricots, roughly chopped

1 Line a 1$^1/_2$ lb loaf pan with a sheet of kitchen foil.

2 Using a sharp knife, roughly chop the almonds.

3 Place the chocolate, butter, milk, and cinnamon in a heavy-based saucepan. Heat gently over a low heat for 3–4 minutes, stirring with a wooden spoon, until the chocolate has melted. Beat the mixture well.

4 Stir the almonds, cookies, and apricots into the chocolate mixture in the pan, stirring with a wooden spoon, until well mixed.

5 Pour the mixture into the prepared pan and leave to chill in the refrigerator for about 1 hour or until set.

6 Cut the rich chocolate loaf into slices to serve.

COOK'S TIP

To melt chocolate, first break it into manageable pieces. The smaller the pieces, the quicker it will melt.

COOK'S TIP

When baking or cooking with fat, butter has the finest flavor. If possible, it is best to use unsalted butter as an ingredient in puddings and desserts, unless stated otherwise in the recipe.

Peaches in White Wine

A very simple but incredibly pleasing dessert, which is especially good for a dinner party on a hot summer day.

Serves 4

INGREDIENTS

4 large ripe peaches
2 tbsp confectioners' sugar, sifted
pared peel and juice of 1 orange

³/₄ cup medium or sweet white wine, chilled

1 Using a sharp knife, halve the peaches, remove the stones, and discard them. Peel the peaches if you prefer. Slice the peaches into thin wedges.

2 Place the peach wedges in a glass serving bowl and sprinkle the sugar over.

3 Using a sharp knife, pare the peel from the orange. Cut the orange peel into matchsticks, place them in a bowl of cold water and set aside.

4 Squeeze the juice from the orange and pour over the peaches together with the wine.

5 Leave the peaches to marinate and chill in the refrigerator for at least 1 hour.

6 Remove the orange peel from the cold water and pat dry with paper towels.

7 Garnish the peaches with the strips of orange peel and serve immediately.

COOK'S TIP

There is absolutely no need to use expensive wine in this recipe, so it can be quite economical to make.

COOK'S TIP

The best way to pare the peel thinly from citrus fruits is to use a potato peeler.

Almond Trifles

Amaretti cookies can be made with ground almonds, which give them a high fat content. For this recipe, make sure you use the cookies made from apricot kernels, which have a lower fat content.

Serves 4

INGREDIENTS

8 Amaretti di Saronno cookies

4 tbsp brandy *or* Amaretti liqueur

8 oz raspberries, thawed
    if frozen

1¼ cups low-fat custard

1¼ cups low-fat unsweetened
    yogurt

1 tsp almond extract

½ oz toasted almonds,
    slivered

1 tsp cocoa powder

1 Place the cookies in a mixing bowl and using a rolling pin, carefully crush the cookies into small pieces.

2 Divide the crushed cookies among 4 serving glasses. Sprinkle over the brandy or liqueur and leave to stand for about 30 minutes to allow the cookies to soften.

3 Top the layer of cookies with a layer of raspberries, reserving a few raspberries for decoration, and spoon over enough custard to just cover.

4 Mix the unsweetened yogurt with the almond extract and spoon over the custard. Leave to chill in the refrigerator for about 30 minutes.

5 Just before serving, sprinkle over the toasted almonds and dust with cocoa powder. Decorate with the reserved raspberries and serve at once.

VARIATION

Try this trifle with assorted summer fruits. If they are a frozen mix, use them frozen and allow them to thaw so that the juices soak into the biscuit base – it will taste delicious.

Red Fruits with Foaming Sauce

A colorful combination of soft fruits, served with a frothy marshmallow sauce, is an ideal dessert when summer fruits are in season.

Serves 4

INGREDIENTS

8 oz redcurrants, washed and
   trimmed, thawed if frozen
8 oz cranberries
3 oz light muscovado sugar

$^3/_4$ cup unsweetened apple juice
1 cinnamon stick, broken
$10^1/_2$ oz small strawberries, washed,
   hulled and halved

SAUCE:
8 oz raspberries, thawed
   if frozen
2 tbsp fruit cordial
$3^1/_2$ oz marshmallows

1 Place the redcurrants, cranberries, and sugar in a saucepan. Pour in the apple juice and add the cinnamon stick. Bring the mixture to the boil and simmer gently for 10 minutes until the fruit has just softened.

2 Stir the strawberries into the cranberry and sugar mixture and mix well. Transfer the mixture to a bowl, cover, and leave to chill in the refrigerator for about 1 hour. Remove and discard the cinnamon stick.

3 Just before serving, make the sauce. Place the raspberries and fruit cordial in a small saucepan, bring to the boil, and simmer for 2–3 minutes until the fruit is just beginning to soften. Stir the marshmallows into the raspberry mixture and heat through, stirring, until the marshmallows begin to melt.

4 Transfer the fruit salad to serving bowls. Spoon over the raspberry and marshmallow sauce and serve.

VARIATION

This sauce is delicious poured over low-fat ice cream. For an extra-colorful sauce, replace the raspberries with an assortment of summer berries.

Tropical Fruit Fool

*Fruit fools are always popular, and this lightly tangy version will be
no exception. Use your favorite fruits in this recipe if you prefer.*

Serves 4

INGREDIENTS

1 medium ripe mango

2 kiwi fruit

1 medium banana

2 tbsp lime juice

¹/₂ tsp finely grated lime peel, plus
extra to decorate

2 medium egg whites

15 oz can low-fat custard

¹/₂ tsp vanilla extract

2 passion fruit

1 To peel the mango, slice
either side of the smooth, flat
central stone. Roughly chop the
flesh and blend the fruit in a food
processor or blender until smooth.
Alternatively, mash with a fork.

2 Peel the kiwi fruit, chop the
flesh into small pieces, and
place in a bowl. Peel and chop the
banana and add to the bowl. Toss
all of the fruit in the lime juice
and peel and mix well.

3 In a grease-free bowl, whisk
the egg whites until stiff and
then gently fold in the custard and
vanilla extract until mixed.

4 In 4 tall glasses, alternately
layer the chopped fruit,
mango purée, and custard mixture,
finishing with the custard on top.
Leave to chill in the refrigerator
for 20 minutes.

5 Halve the passion fruits,
scoop out the seeds, and
spoon the passion fruit over the
fruit fools. Decorate each serving
with the extra lime peel and serve.

VARIATION

*Other tropical fruits
to try include papaya purée with
chopped pineapple and dates, and
tamarillo or pomegranate seeds to
decorate. Or make a summer fruit
fool by using strawberry purée,
topped with raspberries and
blackberries, with cherries to finish.*

Sticky Sesame Bananas

These tasty morsels are a real treat. Pieces of banana are dipped
in caramel and then sprinkled with a few sesame seeds.

Serves 4

INGREDIENTS

4 ripe medium bananas
3 tbsp lemon juice
4 oz superfine sugar
4 tbsp cold water

2 tbsp sesame seeds
$^2/_3$ cup low-fat unsweetened yogurt
1 tbsp confectioners' sugar
1 tsp vanilla extract

lemon and lime peel, shredded,
   to decorate

1 Peel the bananas and cut into 2 inch pieces. Place the banana pieces in a bowl, spoon over the lemon juice, and stir well to coat – this will help prevent the bananas from discoloring.

2 Place the sugar and water in a small saucepan and heat gently, stirring, until the sugar dissolves. Bring to the boil and cook for 5–6 minutes until the mixture turns golden-brown.

3 Meanwhile, drain the bananas and blot with

absorbent paper towels to dry. Line a baking sheet with baking parchment and arrange the bananas, well spaced out, on top.

4 When the caramel is ready, drizzle it over the bananas, working quickly because the caramel sets almost instantly. Sprinkle over the sesame seeds and leave to cool for 10 minutes.

5 Meanwhile, mix the unsweetened yogurt with the confectioners' sugar and vanilla extract.

6 Peel the bananas away from the paper and arrange on serving plates. Serve the yogurt as a dip, decorated with the shredded lemon and lime peel.

COOK'S TIP

For best results, use a knife or a potato peeler to peel away thin strips of peel from the fruit, taking care not to include any bitter pith. Blanch the shreds in boiling water for 1 minute, then refresh in cold water.

Citrus Meringue Crush

*This is an excellent way to use up left-over meringue shells. It is very simple
to prepare, yet tastes very luxurious. Serve with a spoonful of tangy fruit sauce.*

Serves 4

INGREDIENTS

8 ready-made meringue nests
1¼ cups low-fat unsweetened
   yogurt
½ tsp finely grated orange peel
½ tsp finely grated lemon peel
½ tsp finely grated lime peel
2 tbsp orange liqueur or
   unsweetened orange juice

TO DECORATE:
sliced kumquat
lime peel, grated

SAUCE:
2 oz kumquats
8 tbsp unsweetened orange juice
2 tbsp lemon juice

2 tbsp lime juice
2 tbsp water
2–3 tsp superfine sugar
1 tsp cornstarch mixed with
   1 tbsp water

1 Place the meringues in a clean plastic bag, seal the bag, and using a rolling pin, crush the meringues into small pieces. Transfer the crushed meringues to a mixing bowl.

2 Stir the yogurt, grated citrus peels, and the liqueur or juice into the crushed meringue. Spoon the mixture into 4 mini-basins, smooth over the tops, and freeze for 1½–2 hours until firm.

3 Meanwhile, make the sauce. Thinly slice the kumquats and place them in a small saucepan with the fruit juices and water. Bring gently to the boil and then simmer over a low heat for 3–4 minutes until the kumquats have just softened.

4 Sweeten with sugar to taste, stir in the cornstarch mixture and cook, stirring, until thickened. Pour into a small bowl, cover the surface with a layer of plastic wrap and allow to cool – the film will help prevent a skin forming. Leave to chill until required.

5 To serve, dip the meringue basins in hot water for 5 seconds or until they loosen, and turn on to serving plates. Spoon over a little sauce, decorate with slices of kumquat and lime peel, and serve immediately.

Orange & Grapefruit Salad

*Sliced citrus fruits with a delicious almond and honey dressing
make an unusual and refreshing dessert.*

Serves 4

INGREDIENTS

2 grapefruit, ruby or plain
4 oranges
pared peel and juice of 1 lime

4 tbsp runny honey
2 tbsp warm water

1 sprig of mint, roughly chopped
1 3/4 oz chopped walnuts

1 Using a sharp knife, slice the top and bottom from the grapefruits, then slice away the rest of the skin and pith.

2 Cut between each segment of the grapefruit to remove the fleshy part only.

3 Using a sharp knife, slice the top and bottom from the oranges, then slice away the rest of the skin and pith.

4 Cut between each segment of the oranges to remove the fleshy part. Add to the grapefruit.

5 Place the lime peel, 2 tablespoons of lime juice, the honey, and the warm water in a small bowl. Whisk with a fork to mix the dressing.

6 Pour the dressing over the segmented fruit, add the chopped mint, and mix well. Leave to chill in the refrigerator for 2 hours for the flavors to mingle.

7 Place the chopped walnuts on a cookie sheet. Lightly toast the walnuts under a preheated medium broiler for 2–3 minutes until browned.

8 Sprinkle the toasted walnuts over the fruit and serve.

VARIATION

Instead of the walnuts, you could sprinkle toasted almonds, cashew nuts, hazelnuts, or pecans over the fruit, if you prefer.

Granita

A delightful end to a meal or a refreshing way to cleanse the palate between courses, granitas are made from slushy ice rather than frozen solid, so they need to be served very quickly.

Serves 4

INGREDIENTS

LEMON GRANITA:

3 lemons

³/₄ cup lemon juice

3¹/₂ oz superfine sugar

2¹/₄ cups cold water

COFFEE GRANITA:

2 tbsp instant coffee

2 tbsp sugar

2 tbsp hot water

2¹/₂ cups cold water

2 tbsp rum or brandy

1 To make lemon granita, finely grate the lemon peel. Place the lemon peel, juice, and superfine sugar in a pan. Bring the mixture to the boil and leave to simmer for 5-6 minutes or until thick and syrupy. Leave to cool.

2 Once cooled, stir in the cold water and pour into a shallow freezer container with a lid. Freeze the granita for 4–5 hours, stirring occasionally to break up the ice. Serve as a palate cleanser between dinner courses.

3 To make coffee granita, place the coffee and sugar in a bowl and pour over the hot water, stirring until dissolved.

4 Stir in the cold water and rum or brandy.

5 Pour the mixture into a shallow freezer container with a lid. Freeze the granita for at least 6 hours, stirring every 1–2 hours in order to create a grainy texture. Serve with cream after dinner, if you wish.

COOK'S TIP

If you would prefer a non-alcoholic version of the coffee granita, simply omit the rum or brandy and add extra instant coffee instead.

Vanilla Ice Cream

Italy is synonymous with ice cream. This home-made version of real vanilla ice cream is absolutely delicious and so easy to make.

Serves 4–6

INGREDIENTS

2¹/₂ cups heavy cream
1 vanilla pod

pared peel of 1 lemon
4 eggs, beaten

2 egg, yolks
6 oz superfine sugar

1 Place the cream in a heavy-based saucepan and heat gently, whisking. Add the vanilla pod, lemon peel, eggs, and egg yolks and heat until the mixture reaches just below boiling point.

2 Reduce the heat and cook for 8–10 minutes, whisking the mixture continuously, until thickened.

3 Stir the sugar into the cream mixture, set aside, and leave to cool.

4 Strain the cream mixture through a sieve.

5 Slit open the vanilla pod, scoop out the tiny black seeds, and stir them into the cream.

6 Pour the mixture into a shallow freezing container with a lid and freeze overnight until set. Serve when required.

COOK'S TIP

Ice cream is one of the traditional dishes of Italy. Everyone eats it and there are numerous gelato stalls selling a wide variety of flavors, usually in a cone. It is also serve in scoops and even sliced!

COOK'S TIP

To make tutti frutti ice cream, soak 3¹/₂ oz mixed dried fruit, such as sultanas, cherries, apricots, candied peel, and pineapple, in 2 tablespoons of Marsala or sweet sherry for 20 minutes. Follow the method for vanilla ice cream, omitting the vanilla pod, and stir in the Marsala or sherry-soaked fruit in step 5, just before freezing.

Index